Aging With Style

Printed by R.H. Boyd Publishing Corporation
Nashville, Tennessee

COLORFUL MEMORIES: AGING WITH STYLE by Althea Taylor-Jones

6717 Centennial Blvd.
Nashville, TN 37209-1017

ISBN 1-58942-351-8

All Scripture quotations, unless otherwise noted, are taken from the *King James Version* of the Bible, or are the author's paraphrase of it. Scripture passages marked NIV are taken from the Holy Bible, *New International Version*. Copyright © 1973, 1978, 1984 by the International Bible Society. Used by permission of Zondervan Publishing House.

Printed in the United States of America

Taylor-Jones, Althea
Colorful Memories: Aging With Style

The internet addresses listed in the text were accurate at the time of publication. The inclusion of a website does not indicate an endorsement by the author or R.H. Boyd Publishing Corporation. Additionally, the accuracy of information presented at these sites is not guaranteed by the author or R.H. Boyd Publishing Corporation.

DEDICATION

This book is dedicated to my husband, the Reverend Dr. Joseph Jones, for his patience, persistence, support, and encouragement; and to the precious and priceless African-American elders who opened the doors to their homes and hearts to share their *Colorful Memories*. I gained a new perspective relating to my own aging.

CONTENTS IN BRIEF

CONTENTS

Prologue

Colorful Memories is a collection of experiences shared by African-American elders regarding their support, survival, and success while aging with style. At this point in my life, I have experienced many things. For the most part, my experiences in life have been very positive in spite of some seemingly insurmountable odds. Many of my experiences have been quite similar to those shared by these elders.

I have enjoyed intimate relationships with elders throughout my life, particularly during my formative years. Those years were spent in the company of "aged wisdom," namely my grandparents, both maternal and paternal, as well as my great-grandmothers. My own colorful memories include those of my maternal great-grandmother, an intriguing Native-American beauty, and my paternal great-grandmother, an Irish-American saint, at least in the reality of a five- or six-year-old. What a wealth of colorful experiences to be shared!

The memories of those days on the farm, in the kitchen with the elders in my life, motivated me to continue my involvement with elders at every life stage. As my faith in God deepened, I learned so many valuable lessons from my personal relationship with Him and the guidance He sent my way through the elders placed in my path. I learned to reach beyond the ordinary to achieve the extraordinary. I further learned that my success in life is not contingent upon my income but how I overcome. Sitting at the feet of elders taught me to take life one day at a time, to enjoy each moment of every day, and to avoid dwelling on the past and letting yesterday use up too much of today and cloud my vision of tomorrow.

One of the most colorful and memorable experiences I had with an elder was with a devout Christian woman whose husband had recently died. She, in her own way, was attempting to give up on life. She even questioned why God chose to keep her alive since all her relatives for whom she had provided care were deceased. After contemplating on her thoughts and current state of mind, I was inspired to share with her what she meant to me. Once I informed her of my need for her "aged wisdom" and guidance in my life, she gained a new outlook on life. That encounter occurred more than twenty years ago. In 2002, she died at the tender age of 94. While she lived, she regularly proclaimed quite proudly, "Ain't no flies gonna settle on this young lady." She was constantly on the move, traveling in and out of the city with relatives, friends, and peers. She gave me words of encouragement on a continual basis as she believed in giving flowers while one can smell them as well as watch them grow and blossom into full-blown roses. I gained the affirmation I needed for many challenges by her presence in my life as a valued member of my network of supportive others. Her favorite words of encouragement to me were, "Girl, you just keep on pushing, now." What an inspiration. She was the epitome of aging with style.

As I contemplate my own aging process, it is comforting to know that humans are living longer while enjoying a higher quality of life. Quality of life can be positively impacted by engaging in interpersonal connections such as support groups and by volunteering with various service, religious, civic, and educational boards and committees. Additionally, a sound wellness program, including good nutrition and a regular exercise routine, serves to enhance quality of life. I asked my best friend, lover, counselor, soul mate, and life partner, my husband Joseph, to indulge me and do as Browning wrote: "Grow old along with me, the best is yet to be...." I have only just begun my life as a journey rather than a trip. It is my belief that not only does wine improve with age, but so do humans. The support of my spouse, family, and friends will serve to enrich the years ahead. Past successes in areas of my personal, educational, and social life provide fuel for the journey yet to come. Therefore, life in the future can only get better. Thus, *Colorful Memories: Aging With Style* is offered as a road map or guide and as wonderful words of wisdom. Use them wisely and often, and share them with all the significant others in your life.

Althea Taylor-Jones, Ph.D.

INTRODUCTION

Mental and physical well-being is very much affected by how individuals manage the inevitable stressors that accompany older adulthood. A multiplicity of biological, psychological, and social stressors confront older persons. The availability of social support decreases stress and increases well-being (Antonucci & Akiyama, 1993; Hawks, Hull, Thalman, & Rickins, 1995; Lazarus & Folkman, 1984).

Many social factors influence the types of support available to elders and the meanings they attach to that support. African Americans are socialized into a culture of shared understanding concerning what types of support are most effective for reducing stress and influencing well-being (Chatters & Taylor, 1989). Across the life course, these cultural guidelines are connected or blended with personal experience to build an individual system of meaning relative to social support.

Some studies reviewed on family, friend, and church support networks of African-American families indicate that African-American networks and institutions do not simply function as required supports formed as a necessary response to discriminatory practices of the larger society. Instead, they represent a deeply close-knit emotional belief in the value of sticking together (Chatters & Taylor, 1989). There is little apparent appreciation for the manner in which African Americans have creatively responded or adapted to various stressors because these networks and institutions were in place.

Studies on social support have begun to take into account that supportive networks among African-American elders may differ in some important ways from those of other races. Differences are attributed basically to social issues, such as discrimination, that have made the conduct of social support quite different from what is routinely studied in Caucasian populations (Coke, 1992; Coke & Twaite, 1995; Jackson, Chatters, & Taylor, 1993). Patterns of giving and receiving support among African Americans have historically taken place within an extended kinship structure from a perspective of interdependence (working together to help each other) and communal cooperation. African Americans have a stronger sense of togetherness if they are connected with family, church, and social groups which provide some hope for the future and assurance of support in times of need as opposed to being isolated and without hope (Littlejohn-Blake & Darling, 1993; McAdoo, 1995; Taylor, 1986).

Social support is a coping resource. Coping resources are those factors that regulate or lessen the impact of stressors such as life events and chronic strains on mental and physical well-being (Lazarus & Folkman, 1984). Social support acts as a coping resource against many types of stressors (Russell & Cutrona, 1991). Persons with social support are better able to meet the challenges and circumstances of life than persons without social support (Dressler, 1991; Rosenthal, 1986). Supportive relations can serve to lessen the effects of depression, aid in recovery from illness, and decrease physiological and psychological stress symptoms from the losses in life. Loss of a spouse, family members, friends, social identity, health, and other later life issues can be softened or stabilized by support (Antonucci, 1990; Dressler, 1991; Smith, 1993). Social supports are also beneficial in controlling anxiety caused by some mild stressors (Bowers & Gesten, 1986).

Much has been written about social support. However, information is limited on social support of African Americans. Furthermore, the existing information does not address the meanings, beliefs, and past experiences that African-American elders ascribe to social support.

Although much attention has been given to social support, most of the work neglects to take into consideration both the environment within which social support is activated and the thinking processes through which people use and determine the worth of supportive interactions. Many questions remain unaddressed. For example, do the patterns of giving and receiving support written in historical studies of African-American communities have relevance for how support is offered and accepted by African Americans today? What exactly does it mean to individuals to belong to a network of supportive others? What beliefs and commitments influence requests for and use of support? Under what conditions are actions interpreted as supportive? What connections do people make between the supportive acts and interactions of others and their own physical and mental well-being?

In this book, I explore the concept of social support from the perspectives of thirty (30) African-American elders. More specifically, their personal beliefs as well as past and present experiences that influence use of social support are examined; when, how, from whom, and under what conditions support is requested (or offered) is considered; and the positive and negative outcomes of supportive interactions are evaluated.

This book unfolds by painting a vivid portrait of social support and the rewards reaped from participation in networks of supportive others. The book is divided into four parts: Part I, "If You Only Knew!"; Part II, "Life's Lessons"; Part III, "Blessings Received and Shared"; and Part IV, "The Beat Goes On." Each chapter is designed to help readers examine the meanings they ascribe to social support networks and evaluate the consequences of their supportive interactions.

Each chapter ends with a summary and three features: keywords, suggested activities, and Internet information resources.

- **Keywords**—Significant words are extracted from each chapter to give a deeper meaning and richer account of each segment contained therein.
- **Suggested Activities**—These activities will help you to reflect on your own involvement in social support networks and to evaluate the effects of those interactions and/or exchanges on your personal well-being out of concern and love for others.
- **Internet Information Resources**—Various websites and other sources of information are listed at the end of each chapter. The resources provide links to aging services, programs, and social support networks.

Part I includes chapters 1-4. These chapters address the meanings ascribed to social support networks and supportive others. Social support is defined, and most supportive others are identified. Meanings ascribed include the need to establish and nurture close relationships that last over time. Listening, more specifically active listening, and availability rate quite high on the list of meanings. Other meanings include dependability, trust, respect, and passing the torch.

Part II includes chapters 5-8 and outlines the beliefs that elders share. Beliefs cover the domains of family, community, religion and spirituality, and self. Beliefs transcend personal and spiritual realms and include prayer, Bible reading, treating others as one wishes to be treated, mentoring, and providing protection and wise counsel while respecting the privacy of others.

Part III consists of chapters 9-11 and examines the effects of support on well-being from positive as well as negative perspectives. Giving back gives rise to fellowship and blessings. Elders speak of life being more positive because the act of giving results more in blessing than receiving. The blessings of peace, contentment, and joy set the stage for a worry-free life with an attitude of gratitude.

Part IV, the conclusion, contains chapter 12. This chapter addresses three of the future challenges of aging. Further studies are needed that focus on other groups of African-American elders, representing other distinct elements of diversity. Further studies could serve to advance and illuminate colorful memories of other elders who also are aging with style.

References

Antonucci, T. C. (1990). Social supports and social relationships. In R. H. Binstock & L. K. George (Eds.). *Handbook of Aging and the Social Sciences* (3rd ed., pp. 205-226). San Diego: Academic Press.

Antonucci, T. C., & Akiyama, H. (1991). Convoys of social support: Generational issues. *Marriage and Family Review,* 16, 103-124.

Bowers, C. A., & Gesten, E. L. (1986). Social support as a buffer of anxiety: An experimental analogue. *American Journal of Community Psychology,* 14, 447-451.

Chatters, L. M., & Taylor, R. J. (1989). Life problems and coping strategies of older black adults. *Social Work,* (July), 313-319.

Coke, M. M. (1992). Correlates of life satisfaction among elderly African Americans. *Journal of Gerontology,* 47, P316-320.

Coke, M. M., & Twaite, J. A. (1995). *The Black Elderly: Satisfaction and Quality of Later Life.* New York: The Haworth Press.

Dressler, W. W. (1991). Social support, lifestyle incongruity, and arterial blood pressure in a southern black community. *Psychosomatic Medicine,* 53, 608-620.

Hawks, S. R., Hull, M. L., Thalman, R. L., & Rickens, P. M. (1995). Review of spiritual health: Definition, role and intervention strategies in health promotion. *American Journal of Health Promotion,* 9, 373-378.

Jackson, J. S., Chatters, L. M., & Taylor, R. J. (1993). Roles and resources of the black elderly. In J. S. Jackson, L. M. Chatters, & R. J. Taylor (Eds.), *Aging in Black America* (pp. 1-18). Newbury Park: Sage.

Lazarus, R. S., & Folkman, S. (1984). *Stress, Appraisal, and Coping.* New York: Springer.

Littlejohn-Blake, S. M., & Darling, C. A. (1993). Understanding the strengths of African American families. *Journal of Black Studies,* 23, 460-471.

McAdoo, H. P. (1995). African-American families: Strengths and realities. In H. I. McCubbin, E. A. Thompson, A. I. Thompson, & J. A. Futrell (Eds.), *Resiliency in Ethnic Minority Families: African American families,* volume 2, (pp. 17-30). Madison: University of Wisconsin System.

Rosenthal, C. J. (1986). Family supports in later life: Does ethnicity make a difference? *The Gerontologist,* 26, 19-24.

Russell, D. W., & Cutrona, C. E. (1991). Social support, stress, and depressive symptoms among the elderly: Test of a process model. *Psychology and Aging,* 6, 190-201.

Smith, J. M. (1993). Function and supportive roles of church and religion. In J. S. Jackson, L. M. Chatters, & R. J. Taylor (Eds.), *Aging in Black America* (pp. 124-147). Newbury Park: Sage.

Taylor, R. J. (1986). Receipt of support from family among black Americans: Demographics and familial differences. *Journal of Marriage and the Family,* 48, 67-77.

PART ONE

IF YOU ONLY KNEW!

If you only knew! Many things are known; some are obvious and others may be rather obscure. Some knowledge is inborn or hereditary. However, many things through experience are learned…

WHAT I HAVE LEARNED

I have learned—that no matter how much I care, some people just choose not to return the favor.

I have learned—that it is not what I have in life but whom I have in my life that counts.

I have learned—that I cannot compare myself to the best others can do.

I have learned—that two people can look at the exact same thing and arrive at a different evaluation.

I have learned—that my biological family will not always be there for me. In many instances, some people who are not blood relatives have taken care of me, loved me, and even taught me to trust people again. A biological connection is not always the connection that defines family.

I have learned—that the true heroes are the people who perform the necessary tasks, at the necessary time, regardless of the consequences.

I have learned—that I have a choice to control my attitude or my attitude will control me.

I have learned—that I can keep on going long after I think that I cannot.

I have learned—that sometimes when I am angry, I have the right to be angry, but that does not give me the right to be cruel.

I have learned—that the people I care about most in life seem to leave my presence long before I am ready to say good-bye.

— *Source Unknown* —

CHAPTER ONE

WHAT IS SOCIAL SUPPORT?

A classic definition of social support is a feeling of being wanted, needed, loved and accepted by others for what one can offer (Moss, 1973). Cobb (1976) added that individuals receiving social support tend to feel intimately connected to others in their social network and make attempts to reciprocate, return the favor of, the supportive actions of others. Social support also refers to the satisfaction of a person's basic social needs—affection, esteem or approval, belonging, identity, and security—through social ties to other individuals, groups, or the larger community (Thoits, 1982; 1995). In effect, individuals are surrounded by a convoy of supportive others, a group of friends and family who, over time, provide socialization and protection for each other (Dressler, 1991; Kahn, 1994).

As one can see, the idea or concept of social support has been studied since the early 1970s. However, the absence of an application of social support to African Americans, especially African-American elders, is quite apparent.

Cutrona and Suhr (1994) identified five types of social support: 1) informational, 2) tangible, 3) emotional, 4) esteem, and 5) social network. The five categories have been condensed or merged into two broad types of support. The first type, action-facilitating support, consists of informational and tangible aid provided by others to individuals under stress for the purpose of assisting with solving or getting rid of problems. The second type of support, nurturant support, includes emotional caregiving and social network efforts to comfort or console the stressed person without any intent to help with problem-solving. Esteem support can be either action-facilitating or nurturant, depending on the goal of the support giver.

Social support falls into two categories, informal and formal. Informal support refers to support provided by and received from family, friends, church members, and community residents. Informal support is voluntary and tends to be less rigid but activated when a crisis or need arises (Ward, 1985). The composition of informal networks changes with age and unfolds over time. Formal support implies that support is provided by formal agencies such as social service agencies, health service agencies, senior services groups, and general government agencies (Stoller & Pugliesi, 1991;

Taylor & Chatters, 1986, 1988; Walls & Zarit, 1991). Meal programs, transportation for older adults, home aides, and other services planned for older adults are also considered formal types of social support (Johnson & Barer, 1990).

I envision social support as the emotional sustenance and practical assistance provided in times of need by people or groups of people with close personal ties. Therefore, I am concerned with 1) types of problems and beliefs that motivate older persons to decide to seek support, 2) strategies employed to gain support, and 3) types of support that are offered. Social support is viewed as being forthcoming in times of stress or crisis through offers of aid, such as meals or protective feedback that reinforces a positive self-image and sense of optimism (Streeter & Franklin, 1992). Supportive behaviors may also include such activities as listening, expressing concern, lending money, helping with a task, offering suggestions, giving advice, and showing affection (Streeter & Franklin, 1992; Thoits, 1982; 1995).

Perhaps one of the most profound statements ever uttered regarding social support was made by an actively involved, middle-aged, African-American woman, approaching the later years, when she said, "If you can't help me, don't hold me back; and if I can't help you, I won't hold you back."

Sources of Social Support

African Americans typically receive informal support from their immediate and extended family and friends, as well as through their church and social organizations (Taylor & Chatters, 1986). African-American families use the term *extended family*. This term does not imply that all family members live under one roof, but that family members outside the immediate family exchange goods and services and visit each other on a regular basis. Although it is the preference of African-American elders to receive assistance from family and friends (Sutherland, Hale, & Harris, 1995; Taylor & Chatters, 1986; Walls & Zarit, 1991), some African-American elders report more frequent, intensive relationships with friends and church members than family (Dressler, 1991).

Does Gender Matter?

Women report that they use support networks more often than men. Women also report the use of religious coping resources more frequently and willingly than men (Levin & Taylor, 1993). Church memberships are largely female, and women are more actively involved in church activities than men (Smith, 1993). Women and the "oldest-old" (individuals 85 and older) claim higher levels of church involvement than men and the "young old" (individuals 65 to 74 years of age). Older women are more likely to participate in structured activities rather than unstructured activities (Pollard, 1994; Smith, 1993).

More African-American women are likely to be working class and become widows at younger ages than Caucasian women. Working-class women have fewer personal resources with which to cope with widowhood and are more likely to be isolated and lonely than are middle-class widows (Atchley, 2003).

Yes, gender does matter! Both women and men have more women in their social support networks, with women reporting larger networks in general (Antonucci & Akiyama, 1991). Men report that they provide more support to their wives as well as receive more support from their wives, but they report limited involvement with children, other family members, and friends. Women provide more support to a wider variety of people within their networks than do men (Krause & Keith, 1989; Levin & Taylor, 1993).

Gender matters simply because more elders are women. Therefore, women are naturally more available as family members and friends. Additionally, women, particularly older women, have been socialized to provide care and tend to be more involved in providing support to members of their networks (Pollard, 1994). As we age, the difference in longevity between men and women creates gender differences, resulting in female-dominated networks, particularly for those widowed elders who may require more support (Krause & Keith, 1989; Levin & Taylor, 1993). Given this factor, both women and men were included in this study to provide the opportunity for gender differences to emerge and further address the gender issue.

Identifying Most Supportive Others

African-American elders identify spouses, siblings, parents, grandparents, offspring, friends, neighbors, and clergy as most supportive others. Married elders identify their spouses as their most supportive other. Barbara stated, "My husband is always there for me, and he's always doing things that help me. He never says no." Bryant added, "My wife...We have been together so long, we just know what each other needs."

Ralph concurred with Barbara and Bryant when he said, "My wife...I think she gives me [the] most strength. She supports me more than anybody I ever knew. More than mama, dad, or anyone else...When I get awfully quiet, she knows something's wrong, and she calls and wants me to tell her...tell her what's wrong and, ah, of course, I open up to her. Then she tells me not to react but to do it."

Victoria added another perspective. Her husband is supportive and attempts to regulate the amount of stress she encounters, although apparently unsuccessfully. She stated, "My husband. Well one thing, when I'm overwhelmed with the different things that I'm trying to do, he gets upset because he continues to say, 'Well, now you've taken on more than you should be trying to handle,' and he would try to slow me down, but he hasn't been able to do it."

Aging itself can isolate many elders from earlier social networks or bonds. Such isolation may include changes in roles and fewer siblings and children with whom to interact. Physical disability, illness, and loss of independence can increase the isolation. Add widowhood to aging, particularly males in the "old-old" (age 75 to 84) and the "oldest-old" (age 85 and over) categories, and life becomes more difficult. Men who have enjoyed a traditional marriage are faced with the hardship of learning and performing new roles, such as cooking and housekeeping. Furthermore, men typically do not initiate and maintain contacts and interactions with family members. Therefore, once widowed, that link in the support network chain is weakened. Moreover, widowers die ten times as often from strokes, six times as often from heart disease, three times as often from accidents and four to five times as often from suicide as do married men at the same life stage. Women tend to suffer more from economic hardships once widowed (Atchley, 2003; Bee & Bjorkland, 2004; Hillier & Barrow, 1999).

Widowed elders identified a variety of persons as their most supportive others, including children, church members, pastor, neighbors, and deceased spouse.

Bill listed his deceased wife as his most supportive other, and stated, "I come in here to this dining room and sit and talk with her [my wife]. We would talk over our meal and just share our day with each other. I miss that dearly."

Roberta added, "My daughter…She is the only one that I depend on. She sees to it that I have everything I need and some things I don't need."

Arthur proudly proclaimed, "Well, I would have to say it's my pastor. I see him three or four times each week. He was very helpful and loaned me the money without interest to take care of some of the bills that my son left me with from his credit cards and other debts."

Bill placed his neighbor in the family category when he described him. "With no close relatives around, my neighbor is the closest support to me. He fixes up things around here, moves things, sweeps the floor."

The one elder who reported being separated (15 years) identified her daughters as her most supportive others. She relocated from a Midwestern state after separating from her husband. She reported that making friends is not an easy process for her. Most elders tend to believe in the phrase, "'til death do us part." Additionally, the status of separation or divorce is a source of embarrassment or shame for many elders.

Mary, the only never-married elder, identified her most supportive others as "like family." The term "like family" is defined as a person or persons fulfilling a role similar to that of a biological relative (e.g., like a sister, brother, etc.). This is typical of never-married elders who place much value on friends and extended family. Some never-married elders are isolated (sometimes by choice). Others are quite happy and content with being alone and tend to enjoy a sense of fulfillment.

Summary

In this chapter, social support was defined as being wanted, needed, loved, and accepted by others. Additionally, satisfying personal needs such as affection, esteem, or approval are elements of social support. The two major types of social support were listed as action-facilitating and nurturant.

Sources of social support included formal and informal. Formal social support was provided by various social service agencies and programs. Informal social support was provided by family, friends, and other similar individuals and groups, which tended to be more flexible than formal support.

Gender was a major factor relative to support. Women reported longer networks and provided more support to a wider variety of people. Additionally, women, particularly older women, have been socialized to function as caregivers. However, women tended to identify their husband as their most supportive other, with widowed women identifying their deceased husband as most supportive.

Keywords:

Action Facilitating	Formal
Gender	Informal
Like Family	Nurturant
Social Support	Supportive Others

Suggested Activities:

1. Reflect on your definition of social support. Expand the basic definition.
2. Conduct an inventory of those included in your network of supportive others and evaluate the positive and negative consequences of each relationship.
3. Evaluate the influence of gender regarding your decision to request or receive support.

INTERNET INFORMATION RESOURCES:

http://www.AgeWork.com
http://www.asaging.org
http://www.aoa.gov
http://www.eldercare.gov
http://www.seniorservices.org

REFERENCES

Antonucci, T. C., & Akiyama, H. (1991). Convoys of social support: Generational issues. *Marriage and Family Review,* 16, 103-124.

Atchley, R. C. (2003). *Social Forces and Aging: An Introduction to Social Gerontology* (9th ed.). Belmont, CA: Wadsworth.

Bee, H. L., & Bjorkland, B. R. (2004). *The Journey of Adulthood* (5th ed.). Upper Saddle River, NJ: Pearson Prentice Hall.

Hillier, S., & Barrow, G. W. (1999). *Aging: The Individual and Society.* Belmont, CA: Wadsworth Publishing Company.

Cobb, S. (1976). Social support as a moderator of life stress. *Psychosomatic Medicine,* 38, 300-314

Cutrona, C. E., & Suhr, J. A. (1994). Social support communication in the context of marriage: An analysis of couples' supportive interactions. In B. Burleson, T. Albrecht, & I. (Eds.), *Communication of social support: Messages, interactions, relationships, and community* (pp. 113-135). Thousand Oaks: Sage

Dressler, W. W. (1991). Social support, lifestyle incongruity, and arterial blood pressure in a southern black community. *Psychosomatic Medicine,* 53, 608-620.

Johnson, C. L., & Barer, B. M. (1990). *Families and networks among older inner-city blacks. The Gerontologist,* 30, 726-733.

Kahn, R. L. (1994). Social support: Content, causes and consequences. In R. P. Abeles, H. C. Gift, & M. G. Ory (Eds.). *Aging and quality of life* (pp. 163-184). New York: Springer. Krause, N., & Keith, V. (1989). Gender differences in social support among older adults. Sex Roles, 21, 609-628.

Levin, J. S., & Taylor, R. J. (1993). Gender and age differences in religiosity among black Americans. *The Gerontologist,* 33, 16-23.

Moss, G. E. (1973). *Illness, immunity, and social interaction.* New York: Wiley.

Pollard, A. B. (1994). To their memory and inspiration: Women, men and the African American church. *The A.M.E. Church Review,* 354, 32-35.

Smith, J. M. (1993). Function and supportive roles of church and religion. In J. S. Jackson, L. M. Chatters, & R. J. Taylor (Eds.), *Aging in Black America* (pp. 124-147). Newbury Park: Sage.

Stoller, E. P., & Pugliesi, K. L. (1991). Size and effectiveness of informal networks: A panel study of older people in the community. *Journal of health and Social Behavior,* 33, 180-191.

Streeter, C., & Franklin, C. (1992). Defining and measuring social support: Guidelines for social work practitioners. *Research on Social Work Practice,* 2, 81-98.

Sutherland, M., Hale, C. D., & Harris, G. T. (1995). Community health promotion: The church as partner. *Journal of Primary prevention,* 16, 201-217.

Taylor, R. J., & Chatters, L. M. (1986). Patterns of informal support to elderly black adults: Family, friends, and church members. *Social Work,* 31, 432-438.

Taylor, R. J., & Chatters, L. M. (1988). Church members as a source of informal social support. *Review of Religious Research,* 30, 193-203.

Taylor, R. J., & Chatters, L. M. (1989). Extended family networks of older adults. *Journal of Gerontology,* 46, S210-217.

Thoits, P. A. (1982). Conceptual, methodological, and theoretical problems in studying social support as a buffer against life stress. *Journal of Health and Social Behavior,* 23, 145-159.

Thoits, P. A. (1995). Stress, coping, and social support processes: Where are we? What next? *Journal of Health and Social Behavior,* (Extra Issue), 53-79.

Walls, C. T., & Zarit, S. H. (1991). Informal support from black churches and the well-being of elderly blacks. *The Gerontologist,* 31, 490-495.

Ward, R. A. (1985). Informal networks and well-being in later life: A research agenda. *The Gerontologist,* 25, 55-61.

Chapter Two

BIRTHING AND NURTURING LONG-LASTING RELATIONSHIPS

Promoting and Nurturing Intimacy

Do You Hear What I Hear? (Listening)

Being There

The Power of Prayer

Summary

Keywords

Suggested Activities

Internet Information Resources

Reference

To birth is to bring forth and give life. The birthing process is a beginning. Elders frequently talked about the importance of giving birth to and nurturing relationships, and how family and other network members work to create special and supportive relationships that endure over time.

Barbara gave the following account: "I have a niece who is just a delight. We reared her. Her husband left her with eight children, a three week old baby, and ill. Afterwards, she was diagnosed with cancer after he had gone, but she kept those eight children together, and now they are grown. I watched her; she didn't just get down and have a pity party. She said, 'No, I have to raise my children.' They put her on welfare so she could get some help. We helped her as much as we could. But, as soon as she could, she got off, got her a job, went to work, and she said, 'If I do it, my children will do it. I have seen the cycle, and I need to break it.' Now, all of them are grown; all are married except one. I just admire the way that she did what she had to do. Now, her family is taking care of her because they realize what she did for them all these years."

Individuals outside biological families of origin and procreation are frequently included within circles of long-lasting relationships. It was quite striking that elders described the effort and energy they were willing to exert toward and invest in relationships with friends, church members, and neighbors in such an affectionate and accepting way.

Bill spoke of his long-lasting relationship with his neighbor in a very nurturing manner, describing him as a son, father, and friend: "Since my wife died, he's been there for me. He's a tiny bit shy of 60 years old. He comes over; he's been here this morning, and he's like a son, a father, and a friend. It's strange how a person can be all that. As a son, I didn't adopt him as a son, he adopted me as his father. With no close relatives around, my neighbor is the closest support to me. He fixes up things around here, moves things, sweeps the floor. He just moved a file cabinet in the room where I will put my office stuff. I haven't had to ask him for any help. He always volunteers to help me out and do things for me. He came over this morning and put my files in the house, out of the shed in the back, so that I won't have to go out in the weather."

Promoting and Nurturing Intimacy

Nurturing intimacy is perceived as a key element in the development and establishment of a network of supportive others. Nurturing requires one to provide care, encouragement, maintenance, and development. Intimacy and closeness are equated with the generation of feelings of warmth and friendliness. Nurturing and intimate relationships are experienced with spouses, siblings, clergy, friends, and church members.

Bryant shared his intimate relationship with his wife: "My wife and I are very close. Ah, we usually discuss everything with each other. I can tell my wife anything. You see, we support each other and know what each other needs. And, we can tell each other, or we have been together so long, we just know what each other needs. I don't know, I don't know nobody else that I need to go to see."

Victoria added: "Well, I feel very close to my husband. I've always felt that I could talk to him about anything that I am involved in because I've always been a busy person and he has always been a supportive person, even to the extent that when he would work...five days a week...he was a patient person, and it helped me to have patience."

Sibling relationships are close and intimate. Opal shared such a relationship when she stated, "My brother and I are close. I feel a little bit closer to [my son] than I do to my brother. My friends, particularly my female friends, and my sister are also very, very close to me."

People outside biological and immediate families are contributors to close, intimate relationships. Sarah spoke of her close connection to her pastor and in-laws: "I feel close to my pastor. I also feel very close to my husband's first cousin.... I married in the family, but his first cousin, she's close. We don't miss a morning calling.... I can call her anytime. We talk every morning. We call each other. I put it like that. If I beat her to the phone, I call her to see how she's doing. We have already talked this morning."

Friends also are included in intimate relationships, according to Velvet: "Well, I have a couple of friends at our church that I feel very close to. I feel like I can really talk to them and we can talk about the Lord and we can talk about different things, even personal things. [Their personalities are] very much like mine."

Do You Hear What I Hear? (Listening)

Listening is a precious and priceless gift. It is a rare occasion to have the undivided attention of a captive audience listening to you. Listening is perhaps the most important ingredient in the social support formula, particularly when the listener listens attentively, quietly, and empathetically without judging, appearing uninterested, or interrupting your time in the spotlight. Being there by employing the process of listening is a precious gift to possess as well as share with members of your network.

Listening is frequently more important than talking. One can often develop a new supportive relationship by allowing the other person to speak his mind, have his say, bare his soul, or tell his troubles.

Oftentimes, we attempt to listen to others. However, our ulterior motives dilute the intensity of the communication exchange. Yes, listening is a communication exchange, particularly active listening. The listener is then both cognitively (thinking) and emotionally (feeling) connected to the individual uttering the words. Additionally, the listener is responding to the message, not just the words being spoken. Facial expressions and gestures, particularly those involving the eyes, can be useful to enhance the understanding of verbal as well as non-verbal messages.

The eyes of men converse as much as their tongues,
with the advantage, that
the ocular dialect needs no dictionary,
but is understood all
the world over.
— Ralph Waldo Emerson —

Elders described listening as lending a listening ear that goes beyond just hearing words. That is to say, the listener is required to give attention to the unspoken messages communicated while displaying sensitivity—"hearing what I hear."

Positive and pleasant experiences were articulated relative to listening (both being listened to and listening to others). One can speak of and experience the importance of being supportive by listening, not only hearing sounds or words but hearing the needs and feelings of others. Other supportive behaviors reported by elders included such activities as expressing concern, preparing meals, or providing protection.

Jane shared her experiences as a wife who loves her husband for lending her a listening ear: "I love my husband because he will listen to me. He listens, but sometimes, I get wrapped up in something else. But, we have always worked things out."

Listening is vital to all relationships. Emphasis is placed on the importance of each individual doing his or her share. Thus, Lula spoke of being listened to by her husband and friends. She put it this way: "I listen to them, and they listen to me, and my friends, sometimes your friends are listening. But, my husband is always listening to me."

Priscilla and Fanny also shared their accounts relative to friends listening. Priscilla put it this way: "[My friends] are people I can call on the phone; and if I have a problem and want to talk, they will listen to me. They will listen, and they are really just willing to listen. It means a lot in life because oftentimes it is hard to find somebody who will listen. It means a whole lot to me when someone listens to what I have to say."

Fanny added: "I have a friend, and we have been friends for I'd say maybe twenty years, and if there is anything on my mind that I want to get off, I can call her and it is the same way with her. If there is something going on that she wants to talk about, she doesn't mind calling me at six in the morning because she knows that I am going to listen to her as she listens to me, and that is as far as the conversation goes."

Effective listening requires the listener to cease talking. One cannot give adequate attention to another while talking. Another point for effective listening is the creation of a permissive environment. The individual in need of being listened to must be put at ease and feel free to talk. The listener must both look and act interested.

Effective listening is also free of distractions such as tapping fingers, fidgeting, and shuffling objects (e.g., hands, purse, papers, etc.). Empathy is a very important part of effective listening. The listener must put forth much energy and effort to try to understand the point of view of the individual talking.

Patience is a virtue that is required for effective listening. Therefore, adequate time is required on the part of the listener, without interruptions or other signs of disinterest. The listener is permitted to ask questions. However, questions must be appropriate and designed to help develop or express points further. Perhaps the most important thing to remember about effective listening is to cease talking. Effective listening cannot occur while the listener is engaging in conversation. Therefore, we must learn to be quiet, say kind things, and learn to listen attentively. We must remember that God gave us two ears and one mouth. We can interpret that to mean that He designed man to do a double portion of listening. Proverbs 13:3 tells us to be mindful that "he who guards his lips guards his life" (NIV). When we listen more than we talk, the outcome can be quite positive. We not only help others; we help ourselves as well.

Being There

A special connection is established with those providing physical care. However, being there is displayed through just being as close as the telephone, a few blocks, a few steps down the street, around the corner, or across the miles. Stories were not told from a negative or dependent point of view, but from a position of love and gratitude toward caregivers for being there when needed.

Roberta gives this account: "Susie…stays here with me, and she takes care of everything because I'm not able to do it now like I did years ago. Sarah Smith…One time after my husband died, I stayed here alone, and I came down with the flu. Sarah and Mary [her sister] would come up here and see to it that I had food to eat each day and anything else I needed. They would come and attend to me, take care of me."

Family and friends are also counted on to be there. For example, Mary, a retired educator without nuclear family members, draws friends from her network of supportive church members to provide care.

"When I had my surgery, the same friend, I told you we grew up together, she moved in with me because her husband was dead. She lined up a group of people from the sorority, church, and community to come and stay with me while she was at work, and everybody reported on time, and they knew what to do for me. They would take me for a walk, and they would see to it that I was taken care of."

Elders spoke of the care and concern they received from others in their lives who were there for them. Perhaps this statement made by Zennia best sums up being there:

"Your reputation is not established by what you are going to do, rather what you have already done, and still doing. My close friend lives over a hundred miles away but is as close as the telephone. We talk on a regular basis."

The Power of Prayer

The Creator may be approached from many different angles. It is comforting to know that He looks on the heart rather than merely listening to the words uttered. However, for seasoned as well as novice petitioners, discipline is a prerequisite to making an effective connection to the Power Source. According to these elders, intercessory prayer involves a supportive individual speaking to God on one's behalf. Praying is an integral component to birthing and nurturing long-lasting relationships.

Barbara shared the pleasure she derives from her relationship with her husband, particularly by praying with and for her. She also talked about how her church members whom she considers close friends intercede for her. She shared a special intercessory prayer experience with friends and church members after her diagnosis with cancer. According to Barbara, her church members continue to communicate their good wishes for her. "If I say something is wrong physically, [my husband] says, 'Let's pray.' When I go in for an exam, the church members and my friends are all praying for me. They always say, 'We're praying that everything will be all right.'"

Sarah made the following comment regarding how her pastor interceded for her: "He's a good pastor.... He came and prayed and gave communion and all, so I wouldn't trade my pastor for nobody."

Prayer is powerful in any language and culture. One elder shared the following Irish prayer:

May those who love us, love us;
And those that don't love us, may God turn their hearts.
And if He doesn't turn their hearts, may He turn their ankles,
So we'll know them by their limp.
— Author Unknown —

The first formal prayer in the order of worship in many African-American churches is called the invocation. The invocation is the opening prayer in which adoration and praise are the main elements. The purpose of the invocation is to provide a guiding influence to create an awareness of God's presence. An atmosphere of acceptance is established in preparation for communication with and blessings received from God (Jones, 1998).

African-American elders have a rich history of prayer during their worship services, particularly with what is known as "the morning prayer." The morning prayer is prayed openly by an individual, yet others in the listening audience lend support and gain strength from the words uttered. The morning prayer includes intercession for those absent from the fellowship, for the community, and for local, state, and national leaders. Other concerns of the congregation also are sometimes mentioned in this prayer (Jones, 1998).

Prayer is extraordinarily powerful, particularly when one believes that another individual has a close enough relationship with God to speak to Him on his or her behalf. Elders believe that the prayer prayed in the Sunday morning worship service is powerful enough to carry them throughout the week. Making a positive connection is, therefore, quite essential to the power of prayer from an intercessory perspective.

Summary

Informal networks give birth to and nurture long-lasting relationships. These relationships transcend the categories of spouses, siblings, friends, and church. Members of networks strengthen relationships by engaging in active, effective listening without being judgmental.

Connections with network members that exemplify patience, persistence, and genuine concern nurture and strengthen long-lasting relationships. Simply put, network members are readily available to provide caregiving and other types of support. Prayer is the glue that holds together and sustains long-lasting relationships. Network members intercede for one another in both private and public prayers. Intercessory prayer is powerful enough to cover difficulties over distance and an extended timeframe.

KEYWORDS:

Being There	Birthing
Intimacy	Listening
Nurturing	Prayer

SUGGESTED ACTIVITIES:

1. Reflect on relationships that you have given birth to and nurtured.
2. Evaluate your listening skills, and identify strategies that you will use to improve your listening skills.
3. Determine if and when you have been there for others.
4. Have others been there for you? If so, how did the support impact your relationships? If not, what strategies will you use to gain the necessary support from others in your network?

INTERNET INFORMATION RESOURCES:

http://www.asaging.org
http://www.aoa.gov
http://www.elderfriends.org
http://www.ethnicelderscare.net
http://www.seniorservices.org
http://www.visionaryproject.com

REFERENCE

Jones, J. (1998). Examining the concept of African-American worship as pertaining to its characteristics. An unpublished dissertation at Boston University, Boston, MA: Ann Arbor, MI: CMI.

Chapter Three

THE WORTH OF A SOUL

A soul is a human being, force, or psyche. How can one place a value on a soul? When I speak of value, I refer to the merit, goodness, or excellence of an individual. The worth of a soul is further enhanced by being present without judging or wavering and being steadfast and unmovable, even in trying times. The worth of a soul is expanded when valuing the lives of others as your own. Worth is further illuminated by dependability, trust, and respect.

Dependability

According to elders, just being available is the primary component of showing support through dependability. Being able to count on the dependability of supportive others to be available and loyal in the provision of support is priceless.

Barbara spoke of the dependability of her husband: "He is just here for me. We discuss things and we make decisions...pertaining to our lives."

Siblings, friends, church members, and neighbors also are counted on by elders for their dependability to be there for them to provide necessary support. Listen to the colorful memories of the worth of a dependable soul as shared by Opal:

"My sister, we are there for each other, no matter what. In fact, she just lost her son and well, I never even thought for a minute that I shouldn't be right there with her at all times, and that's what I did. And when I lost my husband, she did the same sort of thing for me, you know."

Priscilla concurs with the accounts shared by many elders regarding the significance of dependable people within a support network:

"[My friends] are the kind of people who will, if you have a need, drop whatever. You don't have to wait. They drop whatever and say, 'I'll be there.' I can call in the midnight hour or whenever. 'Okay, I'll be there in a few minutes,' and that makes a difference in some people. Some of them will, you know, wait a little while and tarry, but they respond most immediately."

Dependability is found within the church network as well, according to Mary: "My church is my family, and they give me support because they are right there for me whenever I need them or when they think I want them."

Neighbors are dependable. Bill spoke quite fondly of his relationship with a next-door neighbor: "My next-door neighbor…he has been there for me. I haven't had to ask him for help. He always volunteers to help me out and do things for me."

Arthur spoke of the dependability displayed by his pastor. He stated that his pastor knows the needs of others and the value of being there for them through his dependability: "[My pastor] is a Christian man and practices what he preaches. He is good about knowing what others need, and I am grateful that he was there for me. I told him how much I appreciate his help."

When talking about support, elders described dependable supporters as those who can be counted on (come through in times of need, crisis, or concern) to keep their word and keep their mouths closed or lips zipped because "loose lips sink ships." In other words, when confidence is requested, information shared is expected to remain between the individuals sharing it.

Dependability is a two-way street with traffic going in both directions, yet it has the cyclical effect of a never-ending circle, revolving around the souls enclosed. Charles was elated to share his experiences involving three people who valued his soul and demonstrated confidence in his dependability: "My doctor…I had a doctor to tell me many years ago—I guess he kind of liked me when he got to know me—and he says, 'You know, Charles, I'm depending on you to do a good job where you are.' And I'm asking myself, 'Why would you?' You know, why would he depend on me? And that just kind of brightened me up. Now, here is somebody depending on me to do a good job, so I kind of felt obligated, you know? And I had the same thing happen with my pastor. He said, 'Charles, you know we are depending on you. We like what we see.' I asked myself again, 'What does he see in me?' And then, I had another man who was an influential person in the community, and I said, 'Hey, I need a little money.' He said, 'You do?' I said, 'Yea.' He asked, 'How much do you need?' I said, '$150.00. I wonder if you can sign this note for me for $150.00.' He looked at me, and he said, 'I'm going to sign this note for you, Charles, but you know you have to pay it back.' I said, 'I understand that.' I promised to repay him in 60 days and kept my word. And from that time on, he was one person who said, 'Charles, you know I took a chance on you, but you know what, you proved to be the type fellow that I can depend on.... If you ever need anything, you can come to me.' He is dead and gone now, but I will never forget him."

Friends are sought for assistance usually when the family network, particularly adult children, are not available to assist. Additionally, when specific tasks need to be completed, friends are the primary source of social support. Some tasks include day-to-day companionship and socialization. Friends also are more likely to provide short-term crisis and/or emergency assistance. Crises and emergencies requiring the assistance of friends include, but are not limited to, transportation to a medical appointment, running errands, or other temporary assistance (Hildreth, Boglin & Mask, 2000). Friend relationships are optional, whereas family relationships tend to be obligatory (Bee & Bjorkland, 2004).

Friends also are dependable people as stated so passionately by Mary: "I can talk to my friends about most anything, and we do talk about things. If something happens that I am not quite satisfied with, I have three or four people that I feel comfortable going to, talking to about this, and it is in confidence. I am very careful who I talk to about confidential issues. I just think that if I come to you and talk to you and I say, 'I want this held in confidence,' then I take your word that you will do it. So, I have about four very close friends that I go to with confidential matters. We can go to each other. We came up together, played in the sand, and even made mud pies together."

Brothers are dependable people. They can even serve as surrogate fathers. David shared his description of his relationship with his brother from a mentoring perspective: "I have a brother that all through my life has fathered me from 12 years of age when my father died.... I can think of a lot of things that he has done for our family which developed me and my respect for him all through the years." Elders communicated that dependable friends must be chosen wisely. Friends are chosen for what they are and not by what they have.

TRUST AND RESPECT

Displaying trust and respect within the family unit, as well as within other supportive relationships, is very important to elders. Elders believe that trust and respect strengthen relationships and increase security. Elders further believe that trustworthiness and respectfulness, once established within family members and other close network relationships, can be applied to relationships outside the family and network. For example, building trust and earning respect is essential in casual as well as formal relationships (e.g., communicating with a sibling, passing a stranger on the street, or relating to an employer).

Just knowing that confidential thoughts and feelings will not be repeated to others and being treated with honor and esteem are indications of trust and respect. David spoke of his belief that trust and respect are very vital ingredients of supportive relationships within families.

"Our [family] belief is that mainly we have to trust one another in all we do. We must recognize that we are there to assist each other. If we have problems, we don't have any fear about asking for help. If you would like help and [are] afraid to mention it because you are ashamed of it, you could miss out on getting help. We don't put that kind of guilt feeling on family members that would cause them to be afraid to talk about their problems."

Trustworthiness and respectfulness involve showing honor and esteem for others as well as for one's self. Arthur gives this account: "One thing my mother instilled in us was to respect the rights of others. I learned that, in my family, every adult was to be respected. Not that the children were not respected. But all adults were 'looked up to.'"

Priscilla approached trust and respect from the perspective of individual differences: "I, ah, in my family, we tried to respect one another and their beliefs. I try to pass it on by the way that I live, to respect, respect other people's opinions. You need to respect them and what they believe but not necessarily if it is not what you believe. You respect them for what they believe, even if their belief is different than yours."

Respect enriches others as well as self. Mary spoke of the importance of trust in every stage of the life span: "I think young people as well as people all ages should be taught to respect themselves as well as other members of the family, even the smallest or youngest child."

Trustworthiness is important and an essential ingredient in a friendship relationship, as so aptly stated by Velma: "I have a couple of people who I can go to them and talk to them about most anything. I feel that it won't be something that will be put in the street the next day or tell somebody every time I tell them something. I feel that friends are very important to talk to. Sometimes, we might have things that we would not want to tell the world about, just maybe another friend."

Yvonne shared her belief in trustworthy friends: "I think after living this long time, I believe mostly in trust. Some friends, I have been able to trust through the years, and I value that. It is important to me to be true and trustworthy."

Neighbors are not exempt from meeting the requirements of trust and respect. Perhaps neighbors must display a higher degree of trustworthiness, particularly since their paths cross on a consistent, long-term, and frequent basis, whereas extended family and friends are only required to display their courteous regard on an occasional basis and for a short duration.

Neighbors are surrogate family members in many instances. Neighbors serve in the capacity of a surrogate family especially when family members are separated by distance in miles and, in some situations, distance in emotional investment and commitment.

Bill expressed how important trustworthy community relationships are to him: "I think within the community, I think you should have a close enough relationship that people will trust you, believe in you, and are willing to come to your aid whenever it is necessary. I would not want to experience needing a neighbor and one refuses to come over to offer assistance. That can be a devastating position to be in."

Elders communicated that it is when you trust in the Lord that you can open up your heart to begin to trust your fellow man. Many relationships are weakened or severed because of a lack of trust. Having one's trust violated by another is perhaps one of the most emotionally painful experiences that any human being has to face. Reference was given to the following passage of Scripture. "Trust in the Lord with all thine heart; and lean not unto thine own understanding. In all thy ways acknowledge him, and he shall direct thy paths" (Prov. 3:5-6, KJV).

Summary

The worth of a soul is determined by unconditional love and the absence of judgment, harsh opinions, and inconsistencies. Dependability, trust, and respect are identified as essential qualities or values associated with worth.

Spouses, siblings, friends, parents, neighbors, and church members typically are dependable, trustworthy, and respectful. Thus, these individuals and groups within support networks are considered worthy souls.

Keywords:

Dependability

Respect

Trust

Suggested Activities:

1. Reflect on four situations in which you have been dependable. Discuss the necessity of having dependable people in a network of supportive others.
2. Evaluate the importance of respect and trust in relationships. Discuss the consequences of a betrayal of trust. How does a betrayal of respect and trust alter relationships within a support network?

Internet Information Resources:

http://www.aoa.gov

http://www.apa.org

http://www.asaging.org

http://www.dukespiritualityandhealth.org

http://www.spirituality.org

References

Bee, H. L., & Bjorkland, B. R. (2004). *The Journey of Adulthood* (5th ed.). Upper Saddle River, NJ: Pearson Prentice Hall.

Hildreth, G. J., Boglin, M. L., & Mask, K. (2000). Review of literature on resiliency in Black families: Implications for the 21st Century. *African American Research Perspectives,* 6 (1), 13-21.

CHAPTER FOUR

LINKING THE PAST, PRESENT, AND FUTURE

Passing the Torch

Summary

Keywords

Suggested Activities

Internet Information Resources

Reference

To link is to connect by combining or joining together. One must know where he or she has been and where he or she currently is in order to map out the route to get where he or she desires to go. Simply put, to get from A to Z, one must begin with A and pass through M and N and all other steps in between to arrive at Z.

Elders arrive at older adulthood by first being conceived (A) and passing through the various life stages leading toward the later years (Z). Various experiences at each life stage act as links to connect decades with quarter centuries, half centuries, and centuries, and generations with generations.

Linking the past, present, and future brings positive past events and experiences to mind when thinking about or needing support. A unique concept surfaced that described how elders link the past, present, and future by retaining strong memories of past relationships and interactions with supportive others now deceased. Elders cherished memories of deceased spouses and counted on those memories to keep them focused in the midst of present difficulties.

Opal talked about how she communicates with her deceased spouse about her problems similar to the way she did when he was alive:

"Now that I've lost him, I find myself coming in here sometimes talking to him when I have problems because I don't tell my sister everything and she shouldn't tell me everything. But if I have anything that I want to say, I just come in here and tell him what the problem is. Sometimes, I go to the cemetery and I just talk out what's bothering me. We talked things over throughout our marriage and so I haven't gotten anyone yet that's alive that I can do that with. I just haven't because I don't even do it with my children. First of all, they are not here. You know, I probably would go to my girls and to my son, too. I probably would if they were here, but they are not and I don't feel like getting on the telephone and running up that kind of bill. So, I just talk it out with [my husband] and the Lord."

Bill concurred with Opal when he made the following statement: "It's the memory of my wife of 57 years that comes back to me almost daily, something that she said or did. I think I try not to be morbid or live totally in the past, but somewhere I read or learned that we are a part of all that we have met or of all that we have been, and that thing keeps recycling. I always go back to that because after you have been with someone for 57 years, which is not a short time, many experiences remain with you. I am in touch with reality, and I don't just live in the past, but there are so many things that we did together that I just think about them and they stay with me or keep coming back. They provide comfort and support when I am alone and lonely."

The memory of conversations, acts of kindness, and daily routines of deceased supportive others empowers elders to persist. Exploration of this phenomenon is not evident in the social support literature. The retention of loving memories that link the past, present, and future is credited with providing a source of comfort, durability and focus, not only in daily routine but particularly in the midst of difficulties.

Passing the Torch

To effectively link the past, present, and future requires one to make a meaningful contribution. Effectiveness is measured in terms of preparing the next generation to receive the torch when passed so that they may carry on effectively. When talking about support, elders give meaning to experiences that they have had with elders from prior generations. These experiences are described as lessons learned through supportive modeling, teaching, and instruction by passing the torch. Passing the torch is further described as experiences learned through supportive interactions with parents, grandparents, siblings, neighbors, Sunday school teachers, and other elders from the past and in the present.

Erikson (1982) established eight psychosocial stages of development. He contended that individuals must move successfully through one stage before being able to advance to the next stage. The eighth and final stage is ego integrity versus despair. In this stage, older adults are able to evaluate their influence on younger generations and the wisdom imparted. Typical questions include but are not limited to the following:

1. Did I give my children and grandchildren the guidance and direction that they need to succeed in life?
2. Did I show younger generations the kinds of ropes that they can tie a knot in and hang on?
3. Have I resolved all the issues in my life?
4. Am I pleased with who I have become? Who I am?

Wisdom is evident in the accumulation of knowledge and skills gained by elders over time. This places elders at an advantage over younger generations. Wise elders thereby impart good judgment, sound advice, and unusual insight relative to coping with the difficulties presented by life.

Elders who have successfully negotiated all eight psychosocial stages of development established by Erikson (1982) are a valuable resource for younger generations seeking experience, advice, historical information, and goal-setting, decision-making, and basic survival skills.

Integrity results as the individual progresses successfully through the first seven stages. Despair, therefore, could be the consequence of weakness, helplessness, hopelessness, and/or confusion, particularly when earlier stages did not result in successful negotiation and/or completion (e.g., guilt, distrust, isolation, and self-absorption).

Oftentimes, emotional, physical, and spiritual limitations, particularly illness, influence one to consider self more than others. This decision is in direct conflict with collectivism, universalism, or altruism (unselfish concern for the welfare of others).

Arthur stated: "My mother taught me about caring. I had a doll as a boy that I made clothes for, and I used to knit and do embroidery. That's how I learned to do some of the stitches that I used in my surgery. My Sunday school teacher taught me how to teach others. I taught Sunday school as a result and have been superintendent of our Sunday school for many years."

Thelma corroborated other accounts by describing a close relationship with and fond memories of her Sunday school teacher when she said, "We had a Sunday school teacher, one of the greatest women you can think of, and she dearly loved young people. I had that same Sunday school teacher for I guess about twenty-five years."

Elders equated passing the torch with teaching. They described teaching as a very difficult job that is accomplished most successfully through kindness, observation, warning, precept, and praise. However, the most effective means of teaching is through example. Passing the torch is an activity or tradition practiced by family, friends, teachers, leaders, and other role models or mentors. To pass the torch is to share personal achievements as well as lessons hard-learned with future leaders. Passing the torch is symbolic of lighting an eternal flame. Each time the flame is advanced or passed to another individual, it gains new momentum for the next leg of the race.

Many childhood experiences are quite influential throughout the life span. These experiences are, therefore, ageless. Elders communicated that one should cherish all the happy moments experienced at every life stage. These moments set the stage for the aging process, particularly during later life. Passing the torch is not limited to gender nor stifled by status.

Summary

This chapter focused on linking the past with the present and the future. Linking requires collaboration among members of not only networks but of various generations as well. Elders from prior generations set the stage for today's generation as well as future generations.

Passing the torch is analogous to a rite of passage. Erikson's eight stages of psychosocial development outline a natural progression of continuous momentum from the past to the present and into the future in preparation for passing the torch.

Keywords:

Future
Linking
Past
Present
Torch

Suggested Activities:

1. Evaluate your past and present relationships and link them to the future.
2. Reflect on torches that you have been passed or you have passed to others.

Internet Information Resources:

http://www.aoa.gov

http://www.apa.org

http://www.asaging.org

http://www.elderfriends.org

http://www.seniorservices.org

Reference

Erikson, E. H. (1982). *The Life Cycle Completed.* New York: Norton.

PART TWO

Life's Lessons

LIFE'S LESSONS

To gain insight relative to the meanings ascribed to "Life's Lessons," I explored the beliefs that motivate and define the African-American elder's involvement in a social support network. Elders discussed beliefs as they relate to family, friends, church, community, and self. Beliefs that teach life's lessons include setting priorities, showing care and concern for neighbors, sticking together, and heeding words of wisdom.

CHAPTER FIVE

PUTTING FIRST THINGS FIRST

Many strategies and techniques are used to teach lessons. Some strategies include tutoring of individuals by working one-on-one to convey some message or messages. Lessons also are taught by example through role-modeling. Those elders who teach valuable lessons have taken members of younger generations under their wings and have selflessly devoted time to teach them about support, survival, and success. Simply put, they teach them about life.

Time has not erased my childhood memories of elders teaching lessons about respect, humility, hard work, and fair play. Lessons also included setting goals and priorities. To set a priority is to give preference or precedence. Setting priorities serves to grant the right of way, pave the road for a smooth journey, or give an advantage.

How often do we write a to-do list and enter items on our calendar and/or in our journal according to rank or priority only to change the order because of roadblocks? How often do we just put things on the back burner or on hold until a more convenient time arrives? The best-laid plans sometimes fall short or fall by the wayside.

Putting first things first is communicated when the presence of God serves as a constant force in the lives of elders. Elders credit this belief with offering a defense against the forces that might threaten well-being. The safe haven provided by a belief in putting first things first aids in the creation and maintenance of a positive, healthy environment conducive to growth and development. Elders shared experiences of God's presence in history, particularly during periods of extreme racism, oppression, and other forms of inhumane, discriminatory practices. Joy, peace, and contentment were experienced even in adverse situations by knowing that the presence of God is always evident when first things are put first.

Putting first things first provides a sense of identity and promotes unity. Putting first things first maintains self-worth and mastery. Emma shares not only the benefits she gains from putting first things first but also how she encourages others to do likewise: "I try to live by what I grew up with—that God comes first and that all people are equal in the sight of God. I tell young people, my children, grandchildren, and others that I come in contact with, to keep God first and treat people right. I tell them that if they do right by others, things will turn out right for them."

Violet agrees that putting first things first is a sure way to experience a sense of peace and contentment in life: "Well, with God's help, I feel like I can do most anything, even at this age [87]. I can't do much, but I can do something.

"But, when I was a younger person, I could just do almost anything that came to mind. I tried and I could do it. And I believe that, ah, I was always capable of doing what I tried to do, especially through my church and those kinds of things, or the neighbors or something, I always think in terms of putting God first."

Ralph attributes his longevity to putting first things first when he says, "Well...I, I sometimes, I attribute the longevity of my life to the fact that, if you obey God and do what He has asked you to do, you have a chance to be blessed. Sure, sometimes we break God's Law, but yet and still, He says He's there to forgive you if you confess and try to do better. I will tell everyone that I come in contact with that my total success comes from me believing in God, serving Him to the best of my ability, and that He has blessed me with a reasonable portion of health and strength and longevity. I also tell them that if they obey God, He will do that for them. He won't only do it for one person; He will do it for anybody who loves Him and trusts Him. My dad, mother, grandmother, and granddad believed in God. They depended on Him regardless to the condition or the situation. I do know when they had...the Depression, the Lord took care of all of us."

Velma spoke of how her parents taught the importance of putting first things first to her and her siblings. The teachings included a sense of togetherness, closeness, and safety: "My parents were Christians, very strong Christians, and they taught us. I came from a large family, a family of 12, and we were taught to keep your hands in God's hands, put Him first and He will always be near, and He would always keep you safe."

Bryant shared a story about his childhood struggle with poverty and how putting first things first brought him through trying times.

He also shared his bleak financial situation and how he eluded failure by putting first things first:

"Well, I wouldn't be where I am now, happy and content with what I have. I also believe that, with God's help, you can do all things. Now, I had to bring that in. You can't do it, that, that, ah, has been my story. I believe that I had God's help, and I sought His help and it made a big difference. Now, I can do far more things than I could do without God's help. You see, I was born in poverty, and I didn't have any parents to pay my expenses in school. You see, I had to have faith in God to leave home, go to another state, and enter college. I didn't know how I was going to meet the monthly expenses and all of that. I had to put first things first. [God] has given me the strength to keep going in spite of the odds being against me."

Rituals

Rituals are observances brought about by planning ceremonies and/or following specific, chosen customs. Elders identified rituals as the observance of set practices at specific intervals with the primary purpose of putting first things first by keeping the presence of God first and foremost in their lives. Rituals are described as praying together as a family, praying for others, saying grace before meals, attending prayer service on Wednesday nights, and attending Sunday school and Baptist Training Union on Sundays. Elders listed a variety of individuals as well as organizations that practice rituals. Examples included family, church, friends, and community organizations. Some rituals result in positive behaviors that influence ties with social support networks. Rituals give birth to three sets of beliefs (praying, following family rules, and reading the Bible).

Praying

Elders believe that praying is an important ritual in their lives. Praying is a way of holding communication (talking) with God, petitioning Him for one's self, or commending others (interceding or acting on their behalf) to Him.

Bill communicated, "Every Sunday morning, we would get around the table and have Grace. Mother would pray, and I would read the Scripture. She would include in her prayer every Sunday morning, 'Lord, help those folk who are less fortunate than we are.'"

Ulysses put it this way: "Every Sunday, [families] should pray over whatever they intend to do and bless the house that they live in, the food, their mothers, and their fathers. Praying can help one to be successful in life if they make praying a habit and believe in the power of prayer."

Mary's belief in prayer is so strong that she describes prayer as the glue that helps families to stick together. She simply said, "I just think that the families ought to pray together and for each other. It is and always has been my belief that the family who prays together stays together."

Elders talked about how the ritual of prayer was practiced within their family network from an early age. Velma shared her belief in prayer being the primary focus for all things:

"Well, I believe that a family should be people who should care about one another. The family should pray together. I was brought up with praying in the home. In the morning, we had prayer before breakfast, before we could eat. We also had prayer before supper and especially at night before going to bed."

Violet added, "Well, I believe you should come together and have prayer. The least we can do is have breakfast and have prayer. We all should have Grace before all meals and thank God for the food that He has provided for us."

Following Family Rules

To follow a rule, one must be able to control or manage his/her habits, practices, and conduct. Following rules results in harmony and order. Elders believe that family members should adhere to certain valued family guidelines or rules.

Elders reared their children in the same manner as they themselves were reared. Barbara gave this account:

"I was brought up to pray first thing in the morning before we eat and before we leave home. Before we were allowed to eat, we had to have family devotion. This is the way I was brought up, and it stayed with me all my life. I brought my family up the way I was taught. I taught them to be grateful and to thank [God] because it is God that keeps them at all times. One thing my mother instilled in us was the house rule that the belongings of others were theirs and not ours. We were punished for bothering each other's belongings. Another rule that we were taught was not to steal. She would not tolerate neither bothering the things of others or stealing. If we were disobedient, or if we misbehaved at school, we were punished, unless we had a very good reason. Those rules stayed with me. Yes, we didn't do anything that was against [our parents'] teaching. We would get punished for going against their teaching. They taught us the difference between right and wrong."

Bible Reading

Elders talked about their belief in the ritual of reading the Bible. Moving experiences were shared regarding passages of Scripture that provided comfort in various situations. Roberta shared her coping strategies after her husband died. She stated that Psalm 91 still provides comfort for her when she feels lonely and isolated from human support systems. She made the following statement:

"There is a chapter in the Bible that's the 91st Psalm. After my husband died, I felt that I was all alone. I lived alone, and there was nobody here with me. After a few days, everybody else was busy with their lives. So, I read the 91st Psalm nearly every night because it gave me strength during my bereavement. I still read it each night and can go to bed and sleep peacefully, all alone."

Psalm 91

1 He that dwelleth in the secret place of the most High shall abide under the shadow of the Almighty.

2 I will say of the Lord, He is my refuge and my fortress: my God; in him will I trust.

3 Surely he shall deliver thee from the snare of the fowler, and from the noisome pestilence.

4 He shall cover thee with his feathers, and under his wings shalt thou trust: his truth shall be thy shield and buckler.

5 Thou shalt not be afraid for the terror by night; nor for the arrow that flieth by day;

6 Nor for the pestilence that walketh in darkness; nor for the destruction that wasteth at noonday.
7 A thousand shall fall at thy side, and ten thousand at thy right hand; but it shall not come nigh thee.
8 Only with thine eyes shalt thou behold and see the reward of the wicked.
9 Because thou hast made the Lord, which is my refuge, even the most High, thy habitation;
10 There shall no evil befall thee, neither shall any plague come nigh thy dwelling.
11 For he shall give his angels charge over thee, to keep thee in all thy ways.
12 They shall bear thee up in their hands, lest thou dash thy foot against a stone.
13 Thou shalt tread upon the lion and adder: the young lion and the dragon shalt thou trample under feet.
14 Because he hath set his love upon me, therefore will I deliver him: I will set him on high, because he hath known my name.
15 He shall call upon me, and I will answer him: I will be with him in trouble; I will deliver him, and honour him.
16 With long life will I satisfy him, and show him my salvation (KJV).

Much comfort, strength, and security is contained in Psalm 91. Roberta spoke of how this scripture provided the coping strategies that she needed as a widow.

Barbara spoke of her relationship with and mentoring of young people within her church: "I try to teach them at my church. They know what Mrs. Barbara says all the time. I tell them that they need to read the Scriptures every day if it's not but one verse. You need to read the Scriptures because there are times when you can't get a Bible, and just remembering some words from the Scriptures can be comforting. There are also times when you may be alone or in a crisis or other difficult situations. Just recalling some passage of Scripture from the Bible or what the Lord has to say about situations can cause things that are happening to become less stressful. Reading and knowing the Bible can also help us to reach out to others. And I tell young people to practice memorizing verses in the Bible—because a line, passage, or story can be just what they need at times when nobody is there but you. So, I believe in Scripture reading, not only reading it, but being able to memorize and recall certain passages that fit my situations."

Velma proudly stated: "I was brought up with a Bible. We always had Bible readings in the mornings. I taught my children and other children that I came in contact with to always read the Bible."

Elders spoke of the need to be prepared for every aspect of life. Preparation involved Bible study and knowing the Scriptures to be able to face various situations. Elders also spoke of the need to be consistent with studying the Bible and understanding the meanings ascribed to scriptures. Reference was often made to 2 Timothy 2:15, "Study to shew thyself approved unto God, a workman that needeth not to be ashamed, rightly dividing the word of truth" (KJV).

Elders shared some favorite passages of Scripture that they read and meditate on during various situations and events in their lives:

When you are sad—John 14
When you have sinned—Psalm 51
When you are afraid—Isaiah 40:10
When you feel insecure—Romans 8:31-32
When you need peace of mind—Matthew 11:28-30
When you want and need to give God thanks—Psalm 138
When you are feeling down and depressed—Psalm 34:17-19
When you are floundering and need direction—Psalm 25:4-5
When you are faced with having to make decisions—Proverbs 3:5-6
When you are facing family problems and need counseling—Ephesians 5:22-23, 6:1-4
When you feel lonely, isolated, and alone, particularly during times of illness—Psalm 41

Elders frequently mentioned the Book of Proverbs as the place in the Bible that is fertile with many wise words. These words are very instrumental in directing their personal paths as well as the paths of individuals within their networks of supportive others. Some of their unique interpretations are listed below:

- Proverbs 12:15—A fool thinks he needs no advice, but a wise man listens to others.
- Proverbs 12:16—A fool is quick tempered, but a wise man stays cool when insulted.
- Proverbs 12:24—Work hard and become a successful leader; be lazy and never realize success.
- Proverbs 18:15—The intelligent man is always open to new ideas; in fact, the wise man looks for new ideas.
- Proverbs 19:8—The person that loves wisdom loves his own best interests and will realize success.
- Proverbs 19:15—The man who will not work will be hungry.
- Proverbs 19:22—A kind man can be very attractive.
- Proverbs 20:18—Seek the advice of others before finalizing your plans.
- Proverbs 20:20—Wisdom can be increased by seeking advice frequently.
- Proverbs 20:21—Cheating can result in many material gains, but the cheater must face the music for his negative behavior.
- Proverbs 20:27—Follow your heart and avoid listening to advice that contradicts what you know is right.
- Proverbs 21:9—It is better to live in a shanty or shack than to live with an unhappy woman in a mansion.
- Proverbs 21:13—Stay alert and work hard to avoid poverty and hunger.

Christian Principles

Elders spoke freely of their belief in God and of being a Christian. One belief communicated was that people should practice Christian values, morals, and standards. These values, morals, and standards include treating others the way one would want to be treated. Additionally, the principles assist in the training of children in a proper manner to prepare them for the situations and issues they will face in life. Rather than being part of the world's problems, one who follows Christian principles will become a part of the solution.

Christian principles, according to elders, are essential ingredients to enhance quality of life, promote positive development, and increase concern for humankind. Thus, elders take pride in mentoring and modeling beliefs, customs, and practices to younger generations. The adage "Be it a job great or small, do it well or not at all" is quite profound among these elders.

Do Unto Others

The concept of doing unto others can be defined as turnabout fair play, leveling the playing field, or shuffling the deck to create equality rather than stacking the deck to gain an advantage over others. Furthermore, elders spoke of their belief in assisting others to reach their maximum potential. This goal was achieved by viewing others as oneself (as equals). In other words, promoting a balanced relationship rather than creating a relationship with one on top and the other on the bottom—more or most versus less or least.

Do unto others was described by elders as being fair, just, impartial, pleasant, and courteous as well as having a sense of helpfulness. Elders believed that doing unto others should be a component of supportive interactions with others. The basis for these values, morals, and standards is The Golden Rule: Do unto others as you would have them do unto you. Elders recited and used the scripture Matthew 7:12, otherwise known as The Golden Rule, as a basis for gaining, practicing, and passing on Christian principles: "Therefore all things whatsoever ye would that men should do to you, do ye even so to them: for this is the law and the prophets" (KJV). "Treat others as you want them to treat you. This is what the Law and the Prophets are all about" (CEV).

Elders expressed a desire to treat others fairly. The Golden Rule is the foundation for interacting with others and is a basis for fairness. Interactions are both social and family based. Elders communicated that humans have an obligation to God to think of others before thinking of themselves. The positive message is translated to convey that it is the God-given mandate and responsibility of humans to exert all energies and efforts toward loving and being helpful to others rather than being "nice" in order to be treated likewise.

Elders remained in touch with reality regarding treating others as one would want to be treated. Yet, they realized that following The Golden Rule is a monumental task that is in no way easy to undertake. The Golden Rule transcends relationships with families, friends, neighbors, coworkers, peers, and even adversaries. Fanny explained The Golden Rule as follows: "I try hard to live by The Golden Rule. Sometimes, I fall short, but as a rule, I try to give a person the same break I would expect them to give me. I just try in some small way to show them kindness and that I care about them."

Zennia agreed with Fanny when she cited The Golden Rule as her basis for fairness: "I just do unto others as I would have them to do unto me."

Emma shared her experiences with fairness and justice as the basis for treating others as one would wish to be treated: "I taught my children to treat others like they would want to be treated. I tell and show my children, grandchildren, and others that I come in contact with to keep God first and treat people right and that things will turn out right for them."

Lula corroborated the sentiments of other elders when she said, "I live neighborly and try to treat others that I come in contact with as I would want to be treated."

Do unto others is also communicated as a necessary component for support within fraternal organizations. Fraternal organizations are structured around the extended family concept and designed to provide social support. Quincy expressed the concept of extended family among fraternal organizations: "My fraternity brothers are very dear to me. They are good people, you know. They treat you right and I treat them right."

Jesus...Others...You

Elders used the JOY principle when describing The Golden Rule. The JOY principle is a very effective and efficient way to invest in service with blessings as the positive outcome. The JOY principle was explained as putting Jesus first, others second, and yourself last—thus the acronym: J = Jesus, O = Others, and Y = You. When one keeps Jesus at the top of his or her list of priorities, all other things have a way of falling into place. When the Lord comes first, one finds it easier to think of others before self. Service to others becomes a fulfilling and enjoyable part of daily life.

According to Galatians 6:9-10, we must not be weary in well doing but take every opportunity we have to do good. A harvest is at the end of the toils and trials that we experience. That alone is very assuring.

Train Up a Child

Training is a way to instruct or enlighten others. Training also is used to prepare, guide, or shape others for tasks, duties, or responsibilities. The process of training requires the trainer to show leadership skills, provide encouragement, and nurture the trainee. Elders spoke of moral virtues and contrary vices and how parental beliefs in God led them also to believe that Christian principles should be taught to their children.

Elders referred to Proverbs 22:6, "Train up a child in the way he should go: and when he is old, he will not depart from it" (KJV).

Violet stated her belief when she said, "I believe that we should start training children at an early age. We can't wait until children are too old and set in their bad habits. If you train up a child in the way that he should go, most of the time, he will follow that teaching. He might stray, but he will eventually come back to the training. They will have a hard time doing wrong when they have been taught to do right."

Elders listed ten training rules for children to practice.

The rules are as follows:

1. Uphold your parents' instructions; they brought you in this world and provided for you.
2. Choose friends very carefully; you become what they are.
3. Take control of your habits, or they will take control of you.
4. Be grateful for each day; spend each one wisely and invest positive energy into it.

5. Take a stand for something, or you will fall for anything. Stand up for what you believe in.
6. Select a date that you would take home to your mother and marry.
7. Seek out giving rather than receiving.
8. Take care with your words, thoughts, and deeds; you are how you act.
9. Leave worldly things alone; practice reading and living the Scriptures on a daily basis.
10. Dedicate your life to Christ; He gave His for you at Calvary.

Zennia added: "We must, we must teach our children. We must set an example for them to live by. We must live by that in front of them. You must be kind, and you must always be willing to do something for other people. Don't look for someone else to do something for you all the time. Pass it on and do it willingly, not begrudgingly. Don't ever act like you don't want to do anything for others."

The words penned by Dorothy Law Nolte can perhaps best describe the theme "train up a child."

Children Learn What They Live

If a child lives with criticism, he learns to condemn.

If a child lives with hostility, he learns to fight.

If a child lives with ridicule, he learns to be shy.

If a child lives with shame, he learns to feel guilty.

If a child lives with tolerance, he learns to be patient.

If a child lives with encouragement, he learns confidence.

If a child lives with praise, he learns to appreciate.

If a child lives with fairness, he learns justice.

If a child lives with security, he learns to have faith.

If a child lives with approval, he learns to like himself.

If a child lives with acceptance and friendship, he learns to find love in the world.

Summary

The primary emphasis of this chapter has been to discuss the value of putting first things first. More specifically, the emphasis has been setting priorities and giving God first place in one's life. By putting God first, elders felt a sense of safety and security particularly during past trials and tribulations associated with racism, oppression, and other discriminatory practices.

Elders employ a variety of beliefs, principles, and practices to help during difficult times. Rituals such as saying blessings before meals as well as attending prayer meetings, Sunday school, and Baptist Training Union give birth to other beliefs (praying, following family rules, and reading the Bible).

Christian principles practiced by elders not only enhance their personal growth and development but also assist others in reaching their maximum potential. Two major Christian principles explored in this chapter were doing unto others and training children. Both principles have as a foundation putting first things first—that is, putting God first.

KEYWORDS:

Bible Reading	Christian Principles
Praying	Priorities
Rituals	Rules
Training	

SUGGESTED ACTIVITIES:

1. Reflect on some strategies used to set priorities within relationships in your support network.
2. Evaluate some of the rituals to be practiced and rules to be followed to maintain relationships within a support network.

INTERNET INFORMATION RESOURCES:

http://www.aoa.gov
http://www.apa.org
http://www.asaging.org
http://www.seniorservices.org
http://www.seniors-site.com
http://www.visionaryproject.com
http://www.dukespiritualityandhealth.org

CHAPTER SIX

WHO IS MY NEIGHBOR?

Neighbors are considered people who live next door or people who are residing in proximity (i.e., on the same street and/or in the same neighborhood). Casual acquaintances and strangers also are considered neighbors, particularly in the context of religious beliefs and Christian principles.

Who is my neighbor? Elders believed in showing compassion and concern for neighbors. They expressed an understanding of what others were experiencing (e.g., trials, troubles, and sorrows) from an empathetic point of view. Some of the beliefs relative to concern for neighbors were displayed through watching out for the safety and welfare of neighbors. Elders responded to the question "Who is my neighbor?" by expressing the belief that people within a neighborhood should respect the rights of individuals and property and should look out for each other.

Elders believed that to be able to look out for each other, neighbors must exhibit a sense of closeness. Closeness in turn produces awareness, and awareness begets responsibility. The ultimate action, according to elders, is communication among neighbors with a common interest in the safety and protection of others. As elders spoke of their concern for neighbors, the concepts of providing protection and minding one's own business surfaced.

Providing Protection

Providing protection is the process of looking out for others. Providing protection involves watching out not only for people but also for property (homes, automobiles, lawn equipment/furniture, animals, etc.). David expressed it this way: "Well, if your back porch light is on, I will call and say, 'Well, did you know your back porch light was on?' Or, 'Did you know you left your car lights on?'"

Fanny added, "Well, if my paper stays on the porch too long in the morning, [my neighbor] will find a little excuse to call me on the phone and say, 'I just want to make sure you are all right.' We don't really see that much of each other, but I know she's got her eye on me all the time, which makes me feel real good, especially now that I am here by myself."

Violet pledged her concern regarding providing protection when she spoke of being available to assist her neighbors with any needs that they may have. She also was adamant regarding the offer of assistance and stated that she will try to perform any act of kindness without limitations or boundaries. In other words, she is not expecting anything in return for her deeds.

Having a belief in the concern for and providing protection for neighbors often will require one to leave the confines of a comfortable home and comfort zones and venture out in the unknown territory of the neighborhood in a supportive way. Yvonne voiced her commitment to do her part for neighborhood watch:

"Reach out to each other. You can't know anything about what's going on if you're to stay in your house. Now we have this, what you call this, crime watch program. It's up and down this street in particular. Neighbors just look out for each other. If we see people lying around, you know we alert the neighbors about it. If somebody is going up and down the street trying to sell something, we pass the word and look out for each other."

Zennia added, "This one neighbor who lives across the street from us comes to see me on a regular basis. We call each other. If we don't see each other in a couple of days, I call to check on her, to see if she's all right. If you don't ever visit [your neighbors], you can call up and find out if they are all right. If we don't see each other going back and forth, we check on them. They could be in there sick, helpless, or dead."

Roberta, a 99-year-old retired schoolteacher, put it this way:

"If you are a good neighbor, you have the interest of the neighborhood and the condition of all the neighbors. Likewise, they have your interest and condition at heart."

Elders spoke of the generosity of sharing love and concern with neighbors. Love, according to them, if given generously, is never lost or wasted; rather, it returns to the giver more fully.

Minding My Own Business

As elders described their belief in having concern for neighbors and providing protection, they also mentioned honoring privacy, caring from a distance, and minding one's own business. The degree of support is not lessened by the absence of frequent visitations among neighborhood homes. Support is provided as well as received without, as they put it, "being in and out of each other's houses or getting into one another's business." Honoring privacy is a major concern to elders.

Emma stated, "I think that neighbors should help one another if they need it. Not getting into one another's business, but know what's going on in the area."

Priscilla concurred, "Not necessarily running in and out of people's houses all day long and all of the time but be in constant relationship, maybe by telephone and living in such a way that people in your neighborhood will call upon you if they are in need. If they are in need and call on you, you should be willing to come to their aid. They should also be willing to lend you aid. But you don't have to be in and out of their houses at all times."

Minding one's own business can prove to be an awesome challenge. However, words from childhood have a way of haunting adults, reminding them from whence they have come, particularly aging adults—words such as "It takes six months to mind my own business and six months to leave yours alone." Those familiar words serve to remind elders that there are only 12 months in a year. Therefore, time well spent provides the opportunity for providing protection and minding one's own business, yet caring from a distance while honoring the privacy of others.

Summary

The concept of neighborliness extends beyond the person living next door to include other individuals—not only those individuals within networks of supportive others but those in need of support. Support is available and provided, yet those individuals providing the support respect the rights and privacy of others. Protection also is provided in the form of watching out for people as well as property, particularly when individuals are away from home, on vacation, or during other types of absences. A system of informal or formal community watch is quite prevalent.

Keywords:

Business

Neighbor

Privacy

Protection

Suggested Activities:

1. Whom do you consider your neighbor(s)?
2. Reflect on two situations when you provided protection for someone.
3. Evaluate strategies that you have used to honor the privacy of others and "mind your own business."
4. Discuss the importance of permitting others to exercise a sense of privacy, yet providing support as necessary.

Internet Information Resources:

http://www.aarp.org

http://www.benefitscheckup.org

http://www.elderfriends.org

Chapter Seven

STICKING TOGETHER

Summary

Keywords

Suggested Activities

Internet Information Resources

Connectedness comes from working together. Sticking together involves family members supporting each other and being able to count on that connection. Family roles and rules play an important part in strengthening family systems. Family members often are called upon to play many roles. On occasion, roles change and are thrust upon a family member without prior warning. Roles are established in many families to meet an expectation established by elders from previous generations. Many family roles are based on traditions, customs, and values. Family members provide support for each other, often against all odds. Sticking together does not indicate that members will support other members when they injure others or exercise negative behaviors or actions. However, sticking together does indicate that members are concerned about being positive role models or teaching others how to become positive role models for future generations.

Sticking together is expressed in many forms. Elders spoke of sticking together as showing unity. This unity is displayed in times of crisis, at planned family gatherings, and through various teaching and mentoring experiences. Sticking together also is considered a tradition, family rule, or expectation.

Elders evaluated sticking together as an expression of unity. The following scriptures were shared:

Psalm 133

1 Behold, how good and how pleasant it is for brethren to dwell together in unity!

2 It is like the precious ointment upon the head, that ran down upon the beard, even Aaron's beard: that went down to the skirts of his garments;

3 As the dew of Hermon, and as the dew that descended upon the mountain of Zion: for there the Lord commanded the blessing, even life for evermore (KJV).

1 Corinthians 12:12-20

12 For as the body is one, and hath many members, and all the members of that

one body, being many, are one body: so also is Christ.

13 For by one spirit are we all baptized into one body, whether we be Jews or Gentiles, whether we be bound or free; and have been all made to drink into one spirit.

14 For the body is not one member, but many.

15 If the foot shall say, Because I am not the hand, I am not of the body; is it therefore not of the body?

16 And if the ear shall say, Because I am not the eye, I am not of the body; is it therefore not of the body?

17 If the whole body were an eye, where were the hearing? If the whole were hearing, where were the smelling?

18 But now hath God set the members every one of them in the body, as it hath pleased him.

19 And if they were all one member, where were the body?

20 But now are they many members, yet but one body (KJV).

Nathan spoke of unity when he shared the following: "The strongest family belief is unity. And that unity should have a spiritual base. Unity from a spiritual perspective should be interrelated and interconnected with anything we hear, and everything we do."

Opal added, "We should all come to, not necessarily the rescue, but should anything happen in the family, we should be there first and foremost. We should keep in touch no matter whether we are close or not, in terms of distance. Miles should not keep family from taking care of each other. Families should always keep in touch with one another every week of the year. We try to get together as a family at least once a year for a family reunion. We've been successful so far that we have been able to do it more than once a year, and that pleases me very much."

Listen to Velma's account: "Well, I believe that a family should be people that should be together. I also believe that, if you be together, this is something to be thankful for. My grandmother was a woman that liked to keep her family together and to keep us together. I lived with her for so many years. It was a part of our life to be a family, not just in name but be together and be a part of each other's lives. We were always taught that sisters and brothers should always help each other regardless of the situation; we should stick together. The family that stays together is a blessing. You will feel like you will always be able to go to your brother or sister if you need something if you are close enough to them to let them know that you are in need. We are family, and we always like to try to keep our family close together. Well, you will feel like you are able to go to your brother or sister if you need something. Brothers and sisters should love and support each other."

Elders spoke about the responsibility of parents setting the example for their children. A very profound example was given by Ralph in the following statement: "Well, I believe in, in the family. Families ought to support each other. Our children saw how my wife and I got along, and I think that was an example for them."

Charles concurred with Ralph and other elders when he shared the following account of sticking together: "My family, my mother and father, were very dedicated to each other. Plus, people who are successful, people who seem to be doing okay in life, they seem to be very concerned about and supportive of each other. They don't seem to be apart."

Summary

In this chapter, sticking together was described as providing support through thick and thin. Unity is the foundation for support, even in the midst of disagreements and negative behavior. Sticking together does not include the support of inappropriate behavior; rather, it means being available to pick up the pieces. Parents in particular are expected to take the lead and set a positive example for their children by sticking together as a unit or family.

Keywords:

Responsibility

Sticking Together

Unity

Suggested Activities:

1. Evaluate how you display unity within your network relationships.
2. Define sticking together. Give some examples of how sticking together can prove effective within family structures or how the absence of sticking together can result in difficulties within the family structure.
3. Design a plan to address difficulties that surface; include strategies to decrease or eliminate future difficulties and to reap positive outcomes.

Internet Information Resources:

http://www.aarp.org

http://www.aoa.gov

http://www.asaging.org

http://www.caregiver.org

http://www.familiesusa.org

http://www.familyservices.org

http://www.lcao.org

http://www.nrcd.com

http://www.seniorservices.org

CHAPTER EIGHT

WORDS OF WISDOM

Like Family

Yesteryears

Summary

Keywords

Suggested Activities

Internet Information Resources

Wisdom is associated with knowledge that is enhanced by clear thinking and good judgment based on stability and experience. Many individuals have a wealth of knowledge. However, information gained must be processed and applied before it becomes wisdom. The more one learns, the more he/she finds out what he/she does not know, particularly when the knowledge gained does not inspire others. Elders assigned much value to wisdom and spoke of the significance of listening to their elders for wise counsel. They connected the following scripture with wisdom: "If any of you lack wisdom, let him ask of God, that giveth to all men liberally, and upbraideth not; and it shall be given him" (James 1:5, KJV).

According to elders, valuable lessons pass from generation to generation. These wisdom lessons transmit from one generation to another through conversation as well as personal example. Such lessons are evaluated as preparation for facing the many responsibilities and changes that accompany each life stage, and elders received honor through sharing (Wimberly, 1997).

Childhood observations of wise individuals are vital to decision-making. Some of the reported childhood observations and experiences included children as well as adults. Elders spoke of some wise children they had known. They also spoke of how wise Jesus was as a child who listened to His elders. They referred to the following scripture: "And Jesus increased in wisdom and stature, and in favour with God and man" (Luke 2:52, KJV).

Emma shared her experiences with her grandmother: "I watched my grandmother and other older people, how they set a pattern for us. It was as simple as just being around her and watching how she treated other people. My parents and grandparents, when I was a little girl, helped me to formulate my belief systems. I watched them, and they also helped me to make some better decisions than I myself had decided to make."

Arthur spoke of the wise counsel of the elders in his life and added Proverbs 4:7 as his favorite scripture: "Wisdom is the principle thing; therefore get wisdom: and with all thy getting get understanding" (KJV).

Personal beliefs are influenced by elders throughout the life span, particularly those elders within church congregations—more specifically, Sunday school teachers.

Mary echoed the sentiments of other elders when she shared the following statement: "We were in the Sunday school class, and the teacher told us things that helped us. And from that kind of training, we grew up with Christian principles. And we tried to pass them right along, and we tried to help our young people to listen to what's going on so they would know what to talk about and not repeat idle gossip and things that hurt others."

Mary went on to state that humility, patience, persistence, and obedience are essential ingredients of wisdom. She shared her interpretation of how Jesus commanded all to come to Him as innocent children. She referred to the following scriptures: "And Jesus called a little child unto him, and set him in the midst of them, And said, Verily I say unto you, Except ye be converted, and become as little children, ye shall not enter into the kingdom of heaven" (Matt. 18:2-4, KJV). "But Jesus said, Suffer little children, and forbid them not, to come unto me: for of such is the kingdom of heaven" (Matt. 19:14, KJV).

Elders spoke of the awesome responsibility that adults, especially elders, must face in leading, mentoring, and teaching younger generations. The responsibility extends beyond biological or blood relatives. Elders shared experiences regarding neighbors, friends, and other adults in general; these adults, especially elders, were responsible for *all* children whose paths they crossed. Some wise words shared with younger generations included the following:

- Regardless of what you attempt to accomplish in life, it always seems difficult before it becomes easy.
- Embrace the unexpected! It makes life much more interesting.
- A dreamer approaches life with a positive attitude. Your dreams will come true if you let them because dreamers are known to take responsibility for making things happen.
- Knowledge is valuable. However, creativity and imagination are much more valuable than knowledge because the foundation for knowledge is derived from creativity and imagination.
- It is impossible to encourage others without being the recipient of encouragement.
- You cannot change the winds, but you can direct your sails.

- The door to happiness opens outward. Therefore, the desire to be happy starts within.
- Life is a continuous journey and not a short trip.
- Anything worth having is worth investing much energy and effort into. In other words, you do not get something for nothing. You must earn your right to gain possessions. You must also earn your keep.
- The road to hell is paved with good intentions. If you make a promise, be certain that you can keep it. Empty promises lay the foundation for disappointment and frustration.
- Nothing beats a failure but a "try." Try, try, and try again. In other words, do not give up. And learn to concede with ease.
- The quality of your life depends on the content of your thoughts.

According to elders, life is full of experiences. Many of the experiences are negative and sometimes dampen the desire to persist. Many times, disappointments and/or frustrations will cause one to give in, give up, and even give out. If one has not experienced disappointments, frustrations, happiness, and success, elders urge them to just keep on living. Time and experiences will bring about positive as well as negative changes.

Like Family

Friends tend to be more readily available than family to the oldest-old (elders 85 years of age and older). Friend relationships also tend to be long-standing, whereas family or kin resources tend to decline for this age group more rapidly than friends.

Friendship networks are extremely important to elders. Older adults seek friends for short-term or temporary tasks. Perhaps this decision is made to avoid risking those day-to-day relationships that are of vital importance to continued socialization. However, family and kin are also friends.

Relationships established earlier in life are continued, particularly between individuals from the same group of cohorts. There is an old adage, "Blood is thicker than water." However, kin and family resources decline with advancing age, thereby making relationships with neighbors and friends more plentiful during the later years. Furthermore, friendship networks more than likely have had and will continue to have a tremendous influence on social and psychological well-being. Moreover, family relationships are viewed as obligations, and friend relationships are optional.

Older adults have a choice to make when support is needed. "What" and "whom" are questions that play a large part in decision-making regarding types of support. In other words, what type of support is available and from whom?

When comparing family and friend networks of older adults, it appears that the family network is clearly considered the primary source of assistance, regardless of the task. It seems that only when family members, particularly adult children, are not available, friends (like family) are sought out for assistance. Friends, however, are approached before family for specific tasks. For example, friends and neighbors provide socialization and day-to-day companionship. Friends and neighbors are also more likely to provide short-term emergency or crisis assistance, such as helping out during illness or running errands in inclement weather.

Elders with family members living at a distance rely on supportive others they describe as being like family. Equal value is assigned to biological members and extended or surrogate members of their support network. Simply put, all persons within the network enjoy equal status and reap similar benefits.

A variety of individuals are said to provide support like family, including in-laws, peers, friends, neighbors, and church members. Supportive others are viewed as being available for fellowship, sharing, listening, and encouraging.

Jane stated, "I have three sisters-in-law, and we have never fallen out. We are just like sisters right now and have always been. They have been in my family for many, many years. We are just like that, just like sisters."

Ulysses spoke about his closeness with a group of seniors with whom he shares meals: "I have a group of people that I meet with when I can that I eat with. I go down [to the senior housing complex] for fellowship, and not just to eat but to fellowship. When I get with them, it seems like an extended family to me, and I love them."

Velma spoke of the comfort of sharing with friends throughout her life span: "It means a lot because you feel more comfortable sharing things with [friends]. I really lost a very good friend last year.

We did everything together. We were just like sisters. We told everybody that we were sisters. Throughout our lives, we have always been able to talk to each other about our problems or whatever. If I needed a friend to talk to, they were there. And I was always there for them to do the same thing for them. We just felt like we could talk to each other and we didn't worry about everybody else knowing about it, you know. It was just nice to have somebody to do that with."

For Opal, church members were like family. She shared, "[Church] has been almost like a second family to me. I have been there for a long while, most of my life. The people there are very warm to me and that has been a tremendous blessing to me."

Yesteryears

"Yesteryears" is a belief among elders that the personality of neighborhoods has changed over time and that neighborhoods are not the way they once were. This drama is played out when neighbors do not know each others' names, thereby limiting the interactions or exchanges made between them. Past experiences of yesteryears include going to a neighbor to borrow a cup of sugar or an egg, or asking a neighbor to run an errand or assist with a task. However, those supportive interactions are viewed as things of the past. From this perspective, neighbors no longer visit or look out for each other as they once did.

Arthur shared, "The community as it was when I was a boy is no longer there. My neighbors were very much like parents to me and all the other children in the community."

Velma agreed, "Well, one thing, [neighborhoods] are not like they used to be, you know. You have people coming and going and this is what is so bad about our neighborhoods now."

Knowing neighbors and keeping in touch with them was a strong belief concerning yesteryears. Neighborhoods of the past leave fond, affectionate memories. Neighbors kept in touch even during the process of daily chores and household responsibilities. For example, visits occurred while hanging out the family wash.

Bryant spoke of this bygone experience when he said, "When I was growing up, neighbors knew each other, and they visited each other. Women talked over the fence while hanging their clothes out. Today, the street we live on, I seldom ever see any of my neighbors.

By accident, sometimes I see them going in and coming out. There isn't that kind of community, that kind of closeness now. I have become adjusted to that. Like others, when I go in, I'm in."

Nathan concurred, "The community is not what I would like to see as a community. The community that I know is one I knew when I was growing up as a boy. I knew everybody on the street, and everybody knew me. Community is not today to me what is nor what it can be."

Barbara spoke of the safety and security in neighborhoods of the past when she said, "We were looked after as we went about, as our parents worked every day. All adults in the neighborhood were our keeper and we knew, respected, and were grateful for that."

Zennia concurred, "Things are different than they used to be with neighbors. Neighbors now stay more to themselves than then. Where I came up, we were neighbors. Now, it's a little different. People don't visit each other in the neighborhood anymore. My neighbors over here, I don't get to see them—only when their cars go out or something like that."

Many things have changed over time. Perhaps the passing of time is an excuse for being so distant. Seemingly, the many new advances in technology (computers, the Internet, call waiting, caller ID, call forwarding, voice mail) and other modern conveniences claim the quality time individuals once spent with each other.

Our computerized washers and dryers have replaced the precious, priceless, and powerful over-the-fence visits that elders remember so fondly. Additionally, the hustle and bustle of our jobs and service with various committees and volunteer organizations not only dominate the time we once spent with neighbors but deprive us of quality time with members of our own households and other individuals within our support networks.

Summary

The major emphasis of this chapter was the significance of wise counsel from individuals in influential positions such as leaders, mentors, and teachers. Wise counsel extends beyond the boundaries of biological relatives to include relationships with friends, neighbors, and church members.

Prior to technology, wise counsel was transmitted through one-on-one visits from yesteryears in the form of over-the-fence conversations or front-porch conversations. Wisdom passes from generation to generation. Time and experience connect to create wisdom. Elders not only provide wise counsel for younger generations, but they also share experiences that taught them how to respect the knowledge and experiences of those that have gone before them. Family dynamics have changed with the implementation of many modern conveniences. Yet, wise counsel has and will continue to be a necessary component of all relationships.

Keywords:

Cohort	Extended Family
Family	Like Family
Surrogate	Yesteryears
Wisdom	

Suggested Activities:

1. Reflect on relationships with individuals you consider surrogate family or like family.
2. Compare and contrast your experiences from yesteryears with present-day experiences.
3. How has globalization and modernization ripped the fabric of kinship structures?
4. Does wisdom belong to elderly individuals only?
5. Conduct a self-assessment to determine if you have any words of wisdom to impart to others.

Internet Information Resources:

http://www.aarp.org

http://www.advance.unconn.edu

http://www.aoa.org

http://www.apa.org

http://www.asaging.org

http://www.familyservices.org

http://www.seniorservices.org

PART THREE

Blessings Received and Shared

Blessings Received and Shared

Elders communicated how it is more blessed to give than to receive. Giving is a vital part of their networks. Many elders credited their ability to help others with being much more fulfilling than receiving. Giving was equated with a feeling of value and worth (being needed for self and others). However, establishing and maintaining a network of supportive others was an essential factor for support, survival, and success.

CHAPTER NINE

THANKFUL FOR THINGS BEING AS WELL AS THEY ARE

Elders were asked to evaluate the consequences of their supportive interactions. More specifically, discussions centered on what impact social support from others had on their well-being. Elders described the consequence of supportive interactions as a positive outlook on life with general satisfaction.

A Positive Outlook on Life

To be positive is to be sure and confident. Both emotional and physical well-being were spoken of in positive terms. Elders shared how they were able to progress beyond changes that accompany aging, such as slowed reflexes, shorter footsteps, dim eyes, and loss of hearing. Reaching out to others is a means of compensating for limitations and other restrictions in mobility and independence. The sense of forging ahead in spite of the many limitations is strengthened through interdependent interactions (working together to achieve goals). An old saying from childhood comes to mind: "Two heads are better than one." This opens the door for give and take, fellowship, and blessings to emerge from a sharing perspective. As elders talked, give-and-take, fellowship, and blessings guided their accounts.

The church is one of the institutions of vital importance to African-American elders. For example, some churches sponsor health screenings for hypertension, diabetes, and other diseases, along with providing health education and other educational programs for older adults. Other churches combine spiritual and physical health care and provide the trained staff to plan activities and facilitate service delivery (Hildreth, Boglin & Mask, 2000).

Programs planned by the church can work to support beliefs, experiences, and strengths that older African Americans already possess. When strengths are readily recognized, a means of improving well-being and reducing stress is also realized. Church programs compliment some of the strengths of African-American families, such as an internal sense of spirituality, kin-structured networks, the ability to respond to internal and external pressures, dual socialization (within the African-American ethnic group and the larger society), a strong sense of empowerment, and a strong sense of self. These strengths encourage and embrace heritage, resulting in a display of internal pride (McCubbin, Thompson, Thompson & Futrell, 1995).

Elders communicated a positive outlook on life when stating that this was the beginning of a new day. God has given each day to individuals to use as they please; however, it can be either wasted or used for good. Therefore, the decision one makes is important because this is a day like no other. When tomorrow comes, this day will be gone forever. The desired outcome is gain and not loss, good and not evil, success and not failure. This outcome is desired in order to avoid regretting the price that was paid for this day and to communicate the spirit of thankfulness in reaping the benefits thereof. Yesterday is a cancelled check, and tomorrow is a promissory note. Therefore, today is all that we have. It is the present, and we must learn to live life one day at a time.

Does Social Support Influence Well-Being?

Social support influences well-being. Social support can lessen feelings of distress and contribute to a more positive sense of well-being by protecting health and morale. Both are essential in assisting people with daily challenges. Social support is most critical when people are faced with stress or a crisis. Elders who do not have social support in place are at high risk for abuse, neglect, and a feeling of decreased personal worth (Rubinstein, Lubben, & Mintzer, 1994).

Social support enhances well-being and alleviates loneliness and isolation. Emotional and tangible support includes grocery shopping, leaving phone messages, talking, and other routine supports. Self worth and independence are maintained through interdependent support (Dressler, 1991).

For many elders, well-being is directly connected to the church network and is a general social issue rather than one related to spiritual connections or involvement in church activities. However, elders who use religiosity as a support enjoy a greater degree of self-esteem, personal adjustment, optimism, and reciprocity because social support boosts self-esteem by providing direct assistance in stressful situations. A lack of or reduced social support is both directly and indirectly related to depression in older adults. Support that communicates regard for human worth and the availability of tangible assistance appears to be most critical to elders (Atchley, 2003).

Give and Take

The reciprocal nature of interactions within support networks is described as "give and take." Give and take is considered quite valuable in promoting and maintaining physical and emotional well-being, particularly when extended or surrogate family is involved.

What we give, we usually get back. If we are friendly, we have friends; if we are pleasant, others tend to be more pleasant toward us; if we show kindness, we will invariably reap the harvest from the investment of kindness. A wise person learns and accepts life as a potpourri of good and bad days, victory and defeat, give and take.

Language from decades gone by has a way of surfacing at very opportune times. Expressions such as "hand down" or "turn over" was quite mysterious during childhood. However, age and experience bring things back to one's remembrance. Elders spoke of giving as handing down or turning over things, customs, traditions, and practices to others, particularly those of younger generations.

Thelma, an 81-year-old cancer survivor, spoke of give and take in this manner: "When this tumor got me, well slowed me down, my church members and neighbors nursed me. This neighbor right over here, she was here all the time she wasn't on her job working in the hospital as a nurse. And, my church members were just great."

Victoria added, "Well, me and my husband have always been neighborly and did what we could for others. It has come back to us here lately. I told him we must have a guardian angel or somebody looking out for us. He had his leg amputated, and when he was in the hospital, I broke my hip. Our church members came over and cooked, cleaned, and did the chores for us. Our neighbors collected and put the garbage out for pickup. Now, [trash] may seem like a little thing, but it was tremendous to us."

Elders provide care and share a desire to remain sensitive to the problems and needs of individuals in their neighborhoods and networks. Elders also encourage others to get the best that they can from life and believe that giving influences a positive outlook on life.

Sarah concurred, "I was, now what I do, if it's anybody that I can help, I help. We have some neighbors that don't even want you to come in the door, but there's some that need help. I always get in my ol' tugbug [car] out there and run and do something for somebody. And I always say, if I can help somebody while I pass this way, my living will not be in vain, and that's the way I am. I feel, if I can help somebody, I feel knowing that I can help them and doing it, I will have a good, clear heart knowing that I've done good for them."

Elders voiced the following sentiment regarding give-and-take:

In my lifetime, I hope to develop
Arms that are warm and strong.
Hands that are steady, yet gentle.
Ears that will hear as well as listen.
Eyes that can see and show kindness.
A tongue that will speak words very softly.
A mind full of wisdom as well as understanding.
A heart that feels, understands, and responds with love.

Fellowship

Fellowship is important to a positive outlook on life. Going out into the community to fellowship with family, friends, church members, and peers is a valuable experience. Fellowship has been known to strengthen and still strengthens the person venturing out to interact with and serve others. Ulysses simply said, "Well, the fellowship that I get with dealing with other people and their dealing with me makes me feel a whole lot better than being here alone."

Yvonne agreed: "You can have activities, but you need to get away from your house and fellowship with other groups, with other people. Calling people on the phone, writing cards and letters to people can be good fellowship. Going where people are and being with people is very important. However, receiving a call is also a very good form of fellowship. I've never isolated myself from people. I've always been a people person."

Emma spoke of fellowship in the following manner: "I go to breakfast every morning with some of my friends and church members. I eat breakfast every Saturday with Reverend and Mrs. Green. We have been doing this for years. We enjoy each other's company. Well, I guess that is good for all of us. I just look forward to getting up each morning and seeing other people."

Barbara added, "My health would not be good if it wasn't for the support that I get. When I was diagnosed with cancer, the fellowship was a life saver. Through prayer and encouragement, I gain support. And even when I go for a mammogram, my church members, friends, and family are praying for a positive result. Praying over the phone is good fellowship and support. I always let them know when I am going in for an exam. I had one last week, and they all said, 'We're praying everything's going to be all right.' I received two prayers over the phone before the exam. They all are very encouraging."

For Bill, fellowship is spending time with his Bible study class and his fraternity. He replied, "That little group that meets at noon each Wednesday and my fraternity have helped me to survive, particularly after my wife died. They have been so supportive that I feel better when I go to meetings with them. I actually feel much better all around with these people in my life. My outlook on life has improved tremendously."

Blessings

Elders verbalized the presence and impact of blessings in their lives and attributed such blessings to their sense of a positive outlook on life. Blessings were directly related to support received from others. Blessings were also related to daily assistance and direction derived from Bible reading and nurturing a personal relationship with God. Blessings were also realized through the provision of service to others. Elders relied on and believed in a favorite scripture from Acts 20:35, "It is more blessed to give than to receive" (KJV).

Elders extended this belief by believing that it is in giving that one receives. One of the scriptures referenced was Luke 6:38. "Give, and it shall be given unto you; good measure, pressed down, and shaken together, and running over, shall men give into your bosom. For with the same measure that ye mete withal it shall be measured to you again" (KJV). Other scriptures taken from the Sermon on the Mount in Matthew 5:3-10 and referred to as the Beatitudes was used to express the blessings of giving to others:

3 Blessed are the poor in spirit: for theirs is the kingdom of heaven.

4 Blessed are they that mourn: for they shall be comforted.

5 Blessed are the meek: for they shall inherit the earth.

6 Blessed are they which do hunger and thirst after righteousness: for they shall be filled.

7 Blessed are the merciful: for they shall obtain mercy.

8 Blessed are the pure in heart: for they shall see God.

9 Blessed are the peacemakers: for they shall be called the children of God.

10 Blessed are they which are persecuted for righteousness' sake: for theirs is the kingdom of heaven (KJV).

Bill stated, "I feel like I'm blessed."

Ralph concurred with Bill when he offered the following statement relating to the blessings that he has received in his lifetime: "I can see it's a blessing. It has to be a blessing because there are so many people whose outreach is not like mine."

Roberta added, "You know, the Lord has...blessed me so that I feel there is a constant help every morning as well as every night."

Sarah spoke of the good feelings and blessings derived from doing things for her fellow man. She referred to her giving to others as the source of her blessing when she stated, "I feel good knowing that I've done what I could do. That's where I get my blessings from."

She continued by using Luke 6:35-36 as a basis to support her belief in good works and being blessed by serving others:

35 But love ye your enemies, and do good, and lend, hoping for nothing again; and your reward shall be great, and ye shall be the children of the Highest: for he is kind unto the unthankful and to the evil.

36 Be ye therefore merciful, as your Father also is merciful (KJV).

Mary added, "Jesus said that we must deny ourselves and follow Him in order to receive a blessing."

She continued by stating that the following scripture shows the commitment toward Jesus and toward others that is expected:

"And he said to them all, If any man will come after me, let him deny himself, and take up his cross daily, and follow me. For whosoever will save his life shall lose it: but whosoever will lose his life for my sake, the same shall save it" (Luke 9:23-24, KJV).

SUMMARY

Thankfulness extends to little words of thanks and praise or encouragement. Looking back at one's life reminds one that it is not necessarily the material gifts given and/or exchanged but rather the smiles, hugs, kisses, and other encouraging gestures that enrich lives. Giving freely of those little things to everyone, particularly those within support networks, is perhaps the most important gift one can give. Through giving, one receives.

KEYWORDS:

Blessings	Fellowship
Give	Positive Outlook
Take	Well-Being

SUGGESTED ACTIVITIES:

1. Evaluate your outlook on life. Does outlook influence well-being? If yes, how?
2. Reflect on your blessings and fellowship. Does the giving outweigh the taking? If not, what strategies can be employed to effect a positive change and to increase giving?

INTERNET INFORMATION RESOURCES:

http://www.aafp.org
http://www.aarp.org
http://www.ageinfo.org
http://www.apa.org
http://www.asaging.org
http://www.infoaging.org
http://www.medscape.com
http://www.ncba-aged.org/health
http://www.spirituality.org
http://www.usda.gov

REFERENCES

Atchley, R. C. (2003). *Social forces and aging: An introduction to social gerontology* (9th ed.). Belmont, CA: Wadsworth.

Dressler, W. W. (1991). Social support, lifestyle incongruity, and arterial blood pressure in a southern black community. *Psychosomatic Medicine,* 53, 608-620.

Hildreth, G. J., Boglin, M. L., & Mask, K. (2000). Review of literature on resiliency in Black families: Implications for the 21st Century. *African American Research perspectives,* 6 (1), 13-21.

McCubbin, H. I., Futrell, J. A., Thompson, E. A., & Thompson, A. I. (1995). Resilient families in an ethnic and cultural context. In H. I. McCubbin, E. A. Thompson, A. I. Thompson, & S. A. Futrell (Eds.), *Resiliency in ethnic minority families: African-American families, Volume 2,* (pp. 329-351). Madison: University of Wisconsin System.

Rubinstein, C. J., Lubben, J. E., & Mintzer, J. E. (1994). Social isolation and social support: An applied perspective. *Journal of Applied Gerontology,* 13, 58-72.

CHAPTER TEN

PEACE AND CONTENTMENT

Change and Challenges

Acceptance

Gratitude

Worry Free

Desiderata

Summary

Keywords

Suggested Activities

Internet Information Resources

Elders indicated a sense of peace and contentment with their present status and life stage. Peace and contentment tended to improve the character of elders. Past experiences evaluated as satisfying influenced elders to persist.

Barbara spoke of peace and contentment when she said, "I just feel that life has really been good to me and that my life right now could not be any better at this stage. I am very satisfied."

Howard added, "I have no complaints."

Sarah concurred when she added, "I am satisfied because I know God is on my side. He'll never leave me alone."

Yvonne gave her account of peace and contentment: "I'm not going to worry about being dissatisfied about nothing. I'm just happy. The Lord is good to me, and He allows me to go to bed at night and go to sleep and get up the next morning. I am just happy, and I am very satisfied with what I have, not asking for no more."

Bill gave his analogy regarding peace and contentment by sharing a story. He put it this way: "[I am only] somewhat satisfied because there are things I want to do that I have not done. I want to reach out to help others. I reach out, but I don't think I have reached out as much as I should. Booker Washington was out in the ocean, and he said that he needed some water, and he sent a message to shore saying, 'Send someone out; we need fresh water.' The message that came back was, 'Let down your bucket where you are.' Right down in the middle of the ocean was a stream of fresh water in the middle of the ocean. He had to let down that bucket to save himself and others. Many times, we get in a spot, and we don't know where to go, and we get in turmoil. Let down your bucket where you are. I live by that lesson."

The happiness in your life depends on the quality of your thoughts. Therefore, what one is thinking impacts who and what he/she is. Positive thoughts can serve to increase the frequency and intensity of your happiness. Conversely, negative thoughts result in misery, quite the opposite of happiness, peace, and contentment. Invest personal time and energy in your own happiness. Accept full responsibility for your unhappiness. In other words, do not blame others for your misery. Rather, work to improve your circumstance but not at the expense of others.

Peace and contentment lead one to realize the importance of time, health, and friends.

Yet, a realization of the importance of self teaches one how to enjoy the lighter side of life through laughter. More specifically, one must learn how to laugh at oneself.

Peace and contentment teach one how to accept the assistance and concern of others while knowing how and when to say "no." Additionally, peace and contentment teach one how to express and process emotions appropriately and to accept the compliments of others graciously. Subsequently, positive outcomes of peace and contentment are evident through the acceptance and display of flexibility and the realization that we all make mistakes.

The world will not end when we fail or make a mistake. There is almost always another day and another chance to make a change or a new start. If we strive to be happy for a day and share that happiness with others, we learn something new and experience growth, development, peace, and contentment on a daily basis. By living life one day at a time, we have the opportunity to begin anew each day. The newness of each day is enhanced when we share our blessings with others, particularly those within our network of supportive others.

Peace and contentment are not:

- Attempting to understand and solve the problem.
- Brainstorming solutions under duress or stress.
- Anxiety about an uncertain future.
- Holding on to the past, or harboring and nourishing guilt from the past.
- Trying to change or fix other people rather than focusing on self improvement.
- Gathering and collecting opinions.
- Writing and rehearsing a rote script.
- Falling prey to what others say, think, and/or feel.
- Collecting grievances and looking for things to complain about.
- Influencing others to become uneasy.
- Being a martyr and suffering.
- Blaming anyone other than one's self.
- Harboring grudges and saving anger until later.
- Pretending and living a false sense of reality.

— Author Unknown —

"Peace is not merely a distant goal that we seek, but a means by which we arrive at that goal."

— Martin Luther King, Jr. —

Change and Challenges

Change

"To change is to be vulnerable. And to be vulnerable is to be alive."

— Alexis De Veaux —

Challenges

"Go all the way to the edge. Don't settle for a safe position."

— Cordell Reagon —

Change is constant in everyday life. Life circumstances often require elders to accept and cope with illness, slowed reflexes, diminishing thought processes, and restrictions in mobility. It is essential to positive and successful aging to remain flexible, keep an open mind, and maintain a positive attitude. Elders shared their awareness of knowing when and how to make the necessary adjustments that impact well-being. This awareness represents an adjustment process. The process includes acceptance, gratitude, and being free of worry. Adjustment begins with expressions of acceptance of current status followed by expressions of gratitude for past as well as present skills, and finally the use of strategies for gaining freedom from the cares and worries of the world that could hinder quality of life.

William added a gender twist to changes and challenges when he stated, "I don't let too many things upset me. I just go on because I can't change them. I don't get down about it but face it and go on. We men are the worst when it comes to our health; we don't take care of our health, and yet we cry the loudest when we hurt."

Robert added some humor to lessen the effect of his challenges. He smiled and seemed to gain comfort by simply saying, "Don't anybody's legs hurt as good as mine."

Thelma concurred when she added, "The little pains that [God] put on me, I told myself that I can bear them."

Acceptance

"Start with what you know and build on what you have."
— Kwame Nkrumah —
"I've accepted my reality. I was meant to sound the way I do."
— Kathleen Battle —

Experiences with acceptance extended beyond physical health to include emotional health as well. Elders communicated positive expressions regarding the declines that they had experienced. These expressions related to the ability to change. Elders realized that late adulthood is likely to pose many challenges requiring change. Ulysses approached challenges with a positive attitude when he said, "Well, my feet and legs give me trouble, and other than that, I'm okay. I go to the doctor for them, but I don't let that stop me."

Yvonne added, "I have poor circulation. Now, that doesn't bother me 'cause I don't sit. I'm sitting here longer now than I usually sit. You are supposed to keep moving and take exercise."

Quincy articulated that he could persist in spite of past challenges. He said, "Although I've had a heart attack, had open heart surgery, I think I can do pretty good. I am active." Perhaps he said it best when he added, "I just think that, one of these days, I will have a heart attack and I hope that I do. I hope I won't be sick for a long time. My father had a heart attack. He was working in the garden and around the house and sat down at the table, had a heart attack, and died. I think it was a blessing for him and for my mother because she didn't have to take care of him. I think, wouldn't it be fine if this same thing would happen to me and I try to live so that, if it happens, I'll be ready to go. I think, I think death is a blessing."

Acceptance involved more than health issues. Elders shared some intimate details regarding the need for acceptance after losing a loved one, grieving the loss, facing illness, and preparing for the end of life itself.

Velma put it this way: "I think [supportive connections] are more important 'cause I have lost one son. The other son came a long ways and had surgery, but [God] brought me through all of that. I am very grateful to be here and able to work through things as well as I do. My family helped me, especially [my eldest] daughter. My pastor, church members, and even the doctors and nurses at the hospital helped me. God brought me through, and actually, I feel, I just feel real good about it now."

Elders frequently mentioned their memory and use of the Serenity Prayer as a point of reference and shared the following: "God, grant me the serenity to accept the things that I cannot change, to change the things that I can, and the wisdom to know the difference."

Gratitude

Gratitude was expressed for current status and future hopes and dreams. Ralph and Mary connected gratitude with attitude and offered the following interpretation regarding how our attitude affects our gratitude: "The longer we live, the more it is a reality how our attitude impacts life. Attitude is more important than facts. It is more important than the past, than education, than money, than circumstances, than failure, than successes, than what other people think or say or do. Attitude is more important than appearance, giftedness or skill. It will make or break a company, a church, or a home. The remarkable thing is we have a choice every day regarding the attitude we will embrace for that day. We cannot change our past; we cannot change the inevitable. The only thing we can do is play on the one string we have, and that is our attitude. Life, according to some saying that I remember seeing, is 10% what happens to me and 90% how I react to it. And so it is with all of us. We are in charge of our attitudes."

Roberta proudly stated, "Many people my age [99] can hardly move, and I can move. I can go, and I am active. I do all I can each day and keep going."

Thelma proudly shared her age and expressed her gratitude with a positive attitude when she added, "At my age [87], there are a whole lot of women not able to get out of bed. Not only do I get out of bed, I do my own meals; I do my own driving. Well, I'm having trouble driving by night now because it's the cataract in my right eye, but at the same time, I'm happy."

Yvonne concurred with Roberta and Thelma by making the following statement: "The Lord is good to me, and He allows me to go to bed at night and go to sleep and get up the next morning, and do little things for myself. I fix my own breakfast, sit down and read the paper, and visit my neighbors."

Nathan communicated that our attitudes often influences our gratitude. He shared the following: "The longer I live, the more I realize that the only attitude that I can change is my own. We must, however, remember that we cannot change the past, but we can change our attitude in the present and work to keep it positive in the future. Once something is done, it's done. We are in control of only our own destiny. That holds true for all humans. Each person is responsible for his or her own attitude."

WORRY FREE

"Many people worry, but they don't do anything about it."

— Pearl Bailey —

Worry tends to turn our hair gray, deepen our frown lines, deprive us of our sleep, and cause other problems. According to Bill Cosby, "Gray hair is God's graffiti." In any case, elders share experiences regarding living a worry-free life. Many experiences relate to health issues and the process of aging. However, aging is viewed as part of living and as a natural progression rather than a loss or negative occurrence.

Elders viewed freedom from worry as being able to move forward and leave the things undone behind. Jane stated, "I don't worry about anything. I don't dwell on what should have been or what could have been. I just leave the past behind and keep moving forward."

Mary added, "There are some things that I look back on in my life and wish I had done, and that school is one. I had a dream of starting my own private school. The dream did not become a reality but I don't worry about it."

Yvonne concurred by saying, "I don't complain. I learned a long time ago that a whole lot of complaining is no good and doesn't help."

Violet stated that she would not waste precious time worrying because she would only pass this way once: "I shall pass through this world but once. Any good, therefore, that I can do or any kindness that I can show to any human being, let me do it now. Let me not put it off or fail to do it, for I shall not pass this way again. And I don't have time to worry about what I could or should have done."

Worrying is destructive. It robs today of its strength and breeds sadness. Someone said that "worry is interest paid on trouble before it is due." Worrying about things that cannot be changed wastes energy. Think in terms of a sailboat out on the open sea. When the wind rises, the boat is rocked to and fro. The captain of the sailboat cannot change the wind, but he can adjust the sails. Life is a journey of adjustments. Things cannot be fixed until they are faced. Although elders faced insurmountable odds, they adjusted their sails and faced each day with optimism before trying to fix them.

Elders shared that prayers are answered and can be the answer to many situations, including life's problems. Elders shared how they have learned to pray continually regarding all things in order to avoid falling into sin by worrying.

Philippians 4:6 was used as a foundation for the phrases "Don't worry, be happy" and "Prayer changes things." Elders also discussed the belief and reality that worry is a hindrance and can keep things from changing.

Perhaps the words from *Desiderata* sum up peace and contentment best. The words and the stories contained therein give a vivid picture of the requirements necessary to attain and enjoy peace and contentment in a worry-free environment.

Desiderata

Go placidly amid the noise and haste, and remember what peace there may be in silence. As far as possible without surrender be on good terms with all persons. Speak your truth quietly and clearly; and listen to others, even the dull and ignorant; they too have their story. Avoid loud and aggressive persons, they are vexations to the spirit. If you compare yourself with others, you may become vain and bitter; for always there will be greater and lesser persons than yourself. Enjoy your achievements as well as your plans. Keep interested in your own career, however humble; it is a real possession in the changing fortunes of time. Exercise caution in your business affairs; for the world is full of trickery. But let this not blind you to what virtue there is; many persons strive for high ideals; and everywhere life is full of heroism. Be yourself. Especially, do not feign affection. Neither be cynical about love; for in the face of all aridity and disenchantment it is perennial as the grass. Take kindly the counsel of the years, gracefully surrendering the things of youth. Nurture strength of spirit to shield you in sudden misfortune. But do not distress yourself with dark imaginings. Many fears are born of fatigue and loneliness. Beyond a wholesome discipline, be gentle with yourself. You are a child of the universe, no less than the trees and the stars; you have a right to be here. And whether or not it is clear to you, no doubt the universe is unfolding as it should. Therefore be at peace with God, whatever you conceive Him to be, and whatever your labors and aspirations, in the noisy confusion of life keep peace with your soul. With all its sham, drudgery, and broken dreams, it is still a beautiful world. Be careful. Strive to be happy.

—Max Ehrmann, 1927

Summary

Expressions of peace and contentment are expressed from a positive perspective, even in the midst of change and challenges. Although many changes and challenges are evident throughout life, learning how to accept them is an important factor. One's attitude is a key component for achieving peace and contentment and is a measuring stick for gratitude and moving through challenging situations without giving in to worry.

Keywords:

Acceptance	Attitude
Change	Challenges
Confusion	Contentment
Gratitude	Peace
Worry	

Suggested Activities:

1. Reflect on a time when you were in the midst of confusion. How did you respond to the challenges presented?
2. Revisit a moment of peace. Evaluate your sense of acceptance and gratitude for the situation(s) you faced.
3. What feelings were generated during your time(s) of peace and contentment?
4. Discuss how worrying about things that cannot be controlled or changed affects one's state of peace and contentment.

Internet Information Resources:

http://www.aarp.org

http://www.AgeWork.com

http://www.apa.org

http://www.asaging.org

http://www.eldercare.gov

http://www.elderfriends.org

http://www.seniorworld.com

CHAPTER ELEVEN

PRIDE AND JOY

Pride

Joy

Summary

Keywords

Suggested Activities

Internet Information Resources

Pride and joy involve gaining a sense of worth and merit from past and present supportive experiences. This sentiment is communicated in spite of some seemingly insurmountable odds, obstacles, and pitfalls. The joy of pride generates the feeling of an obligation to give thanks for what has been accomplished mainly by giving back to others.

Pride

Roberta, a young-at-heart woman of 99 years of age, spoke of her love for children and how she taught school for 45 years. She also talked about how she organized a community club for the children in her neighborhood. She planned monthly meetings and birthday parties for all the children. She purchased birthday gifts and party supplies. She spoke with great pride, and the excitement in her voice was very evident: "I bought Bibles for the children and assigned them scriptures to read. I expect them to be able to discuss what they read when they attend follow-up sessions with me."

Roberta also spoke with great pride when she talked about her recent visit to an elementary school to share with seven- and eight-year-old children her childhood school experiences. The pride she enjoyed illuminated quite obviously as she recalled her experiences working with the Girl Scouts and children at her church. Regarding current accomplishments, she continued by saying: "I take care of my room and anything else I want to do. I got up this morning and made my coffee."

Service to others initiated a sense of pride and joy, particularly through volunteering in a cancer unit at a local medical center, coordinating transportation, working on cars as a mechanic, and other forms of giving back while remaining worry free.

Thelma proudly articulated, "I am a cancer survivor and want to help other cancer patients. I give the patients on the unit what they need but not necessarily what they want. When the Lord gets ready for me, He's going to have to bring somebody with Him. I will be too busy to stop and go willingly. I tell people to get up off their stool of doing nothing and get busy. Don't tell me what you can't do until you try to do for yourself. You can't just sit around and wait for things to fall in your lap. You must be busy doing for others. I kept foster children; I took in the strays and those that others didn't want."

JOY

Joy showed very vividly on William's face when he spoke of his service to others. He uttered the following statement:

"I am actively involved in my church. I am the coordinator of transportation and arrange transportation for church members to attend doctor's appointments and other appointments that they need to go to. I also deliver meals to shut-in people and coordinate a Meals-on-Wheels site. I have been doing that since I retired 18 years ago."

Howard found joy in doing good deeds for others. He stated, "I keep my cars, and I work on my nieces' cars for them. I also go up to the service station where I worked and help out sometimes."

Nathan, a retired corporate executive, now owns his own business and is working full-time as a financial consultant. He spoke of the joy he enjoyed from his accomplishments. Self-confidence filled the room as he communicated how others could be successful with the exertion of a little energy and effort. He shared his formula for success: "I took advantage of opportunities throughout my life that resulted in financial independence. I worked and helped others to become financially independent. I believe that one can control their destiny by rising above their situations and circumstances."

Life seemed to be on the move in a positive manner for Priscilla after working for more than four decades as a factory worker. She had a desire to earn a college degree. However, her life took another direction. She maintained active involvement in her family, church, and community while achieving her goals and finding joy in her accomplishments. She was able to let go of a supportive other, her husband, but thrived on the loving memories that she continued to cherish after his death. Additionally, she reached into her reserve of self-worth, which guided her decision to become a supportive other through active involvement in the community. Her involvement was her way of giving back. She crafted the following account:

"Well, I guess I have always had a desire to be independent and have goals. I worked toward that end even though I did not reach the goals that I set. I had a desire at one time to go to college. In fact, I sent in applications for college but never went. Sometime along the way, you get turned away from things that you want to do. I think it was the desire to do the best that I could in whatever situation I found myself in. Therefore, I always did the best that I could in whatever job or situation I was in. I always took my work seriously. My employers never came to me and asked me to do a job for them. Instead, I always sought out my employers, and once I got the job, I worked hard. I am a volunteer for several organizations in the community, including my church. I am also on call as a bus driver for a local university."

Summary

The elements of pride and joy do not include vanity or self-elevating behavior. This concept of pride tends to be driven by one's sense of personal value and worth regarding accomplishments and sharing with others. Elders shared many positive experiences that resulted in pride as well as joy. For these elders, the greatest personal and positive examples of pride and joy were linked to taking advantage of opportunities that were presented to them.

Keywords:

Joy Pride

Suggested Activities:

1. Develop a scenario involving pride. Discuss possible positive and negative outcomes.
2. Reflect on a situation when you experienced joy. Describe the steps included in the process.

Internet Information Resources:

http://www.aarp.org

http://www.agework.com

http://www.apa.org

http://www.dukespiritualityandhealth.org

http://www.elderfriends.org

http://www.medscape.com

PART FOUR

THE BEAT GOES ON

CHAPTER 12
Future Challenges to Aging

The Beat Goes On

The beat goes on…In many instances, the more things change, the more they remain the same. The fastest-growing segment of the population is the oldest-old (those elders age 85 and older). However, the most powerful segment of the population is the baby boomer generation (individuals born between 1946 and 1964). Those movers and shakers are presently in the age range of 43-61. This segment of the population is marching to the beat of different drums, including higher educational attainment, higher socioeconomic status, more frequent home and other property ownership, and the ability to effect many changes. Demands will continue to increase in all aspects of life. Therefore, the beat must go on and include research studies, programs, and other goods and services.

CHAPTER TWELVE

FUTURE CHALLENGES TO AGING

Keywords

Suggested Activities

Internet Information Resources

References

Elders are able to develop, implement, and manage a cadre of routine and strategic supportive interactions, a unique belief system, and a priceless, positive outlook on life. Supportive interactions, beliefs, and positive well-being are invaluable assets to support, survival, and success.

Many African-American families have overcome a variety of challenges and stressors (e.g., discrimination, poverty) presented on a daily basis (Pollard, 1995). This was evident with the surveyed group of elders. Furthermore, some studies acknowledge the strength of African-American families and maintain that their resilience is relative to supportive interactions that create and foster a positive sense of family unity. Elders communicate that family unity requires a belief in the importance of family connectedness (McCubbin, Thompson, Thompson, & Futrell, 1995). The strength of relationships may be related to a three-fold commitment to faith, family, and community and the teamwork or partnership approach that emerges from intimate connections (e.g., togetherness and showing unconditional love).

Many African-American families have strengths from which they can draw, but few studies have been conducted regarding their strengths (Hildreth, Boglin, & Mask, 2000). These elders draw upon the strengths within both their immediate and extended families, which extends the potential number of caregivers and network members. Flexibility within African-American families is a source of strength and stability. Some sources of strength are supportive networks, role flexibility, strong religious connections, the availability and employment of extended family supports, and use of fictive kin-like family (Hildreth, Boglin, & Mask, 2000). Elders communicated a sense of belonging, intimate connections, and reciprocal support within their families, friends, church, and community networks.

By the year 2030, aging Baby Boomers will make up more than twenty percent of the total population. African Americans are included in that number. Furthermore, aging minorities will comprise the largest group of all elders (Atchley, 2003; Bee & Bjorkland, 2004). Given the increasing number of African-American elders, the need to evaluate the consequences of supportive interactions seems particularly relevant to this group because of the lack of prior studies.

Although conclusions cannot be generalized to include all African-American elders, the level of positive well-being experienced by these elders is enhanced by a combination of meanings, beliefs, and positive consequences of supportive interactions. Elders are involved as both givers and receivers of support and described both giving and receiving as having contributed to their outlook on life and sense of positive well-being.

Some African Americans may have stronger family ties than other ethnic groups, and this factor may have a significant impact upon their social supports and general satisfaction with life (McCubbin, Thompson, Thompson, & Futrell, 1995). It is evident that these elders give meaning to and draw upon their beliefs and evaluate their supportive interactions by consistently employing a variety of strategies that contribute to positive well-being. Many of their supportive relationships and networks have endured for more than eight decades. Living eighty plus years is an enormous feat to imagine.

Three major challenges are presented for the future:

1. The first challenge will be the use of representative samples of elderly African Americans. Replicating this study with persons identified with other cultures, geographic locations, socioeconomic statuses, educational attainment, and religious preferences could prove to be most relevant as well as informative for family scholars, family practitioners, aging service providers, and aging individuals themselves. Contributions to literature about African Americans are needed that do not improperly generalize, stigmatize, or pathologize ethnic minority families, particularly ethnic minority elders.
2. A second challenge for the future will be to expand the definition of social support to include the loving memories of supportive others now deceased. Elders clearly found comfort in the words and deeds of departed loved ones. In many instances, loving memories of deceased loved ones were the main, and sometimes the only, strong support for elders. This perspective has not been addressed or defined in previous studies.
3. A third challenge is to extend the definition of family as it is currently used in the social support literature. Family, particularly for these elders, has been defined as going beyond biological ties to include friends, church members, and neighbors.

Furthermore, the concept of neighbor as defined by these elders was somewhat unsettling. Neighbors were credited with many supportive actions but were viewed as negligent in other ways. Elders clearly were struggling with their beliefs about how neighbors should behave as guardians, caregivers, and educators of the community.

Perhaps the effects of aging might differ for a population that has a different level of economic, physical, or emotional stress. The meanings and effects of aging might well differ under more extreme circumstances.

Summary

Granted, this book cannot be used to generalize all African-American elders 70 years of age and older, but it does paint a clear portrait of social support among this group of elders and contains a generous collection of colorful memories.

Keywords:

Aging	Challenges
Flexibility	Future

Suggested Activities:

1. How do you view your own aging?
2. Evaluate the aging challenges that you have faced transitioning from one life stage to the next (i.e., young adulthood, middle adulthood, and older adulthood).
3. Describe how you will help others face their aging from a positive perspective.

Internet Information Resources:

http://www.aoa.gov
http://www.arthritis.org
http://www.asaging.org
http://www.dukespiritualityandhealth.org
http://www.eldercare.gov
http://www.elderfriends.org
http://www.gero.org
http://www.ncba-aged.org/health
http://www.nrcd.com
http://www.rcgd.isr.umich.edu/prba/perspectives
http://www.usda.gov

REFERENCES

Atchley, R. C. (2003). *Social forces and aging: An introduction to social gerontology* (9th ed.). Belmont, CA: Wadsworth.

Bee, H. L., & Bjorkland, B. R. (2004). *The journey of adulthood* (5th ed.). Upper Saddle River, NJ: Pearson Prentice Hall.

Hildreth, G. J., Boglin, M. L., & Mask, K. (2000). Review of literature on resiliency in Black families: Implications for the 21st Century. *African American Research Perspectives,* 6 (1), 13-21.

McCubbin, H. I., Futrell, J. A., Thompson, E. A., & Thompson, A. I. (1995). Resilient families in an ethnic and cultural context. In H. I. McCubbin, E. A. Thompson, A. I. Thompson, & J. A. Futrell (Eds.), *Resilience in ethnic minority families: African-American Families,* Volume 2, (pp. 329-351). Madison: University of Wisconsin System.

Pollard, A. B. (1995, November). Race, religion, and resistance in the African American experience. Paper presented at the Associacao Nacional Casa Dandara International Seminar, Minas Gerais, Brazil.

EPILOGUE

The primary purpose of this book was to address the social support networks of African-American elders; more specifically, persons considered as supportive others, meanings ascribed to relationships, beliefs that motivated use of support, and how support affected well-being. The aim of this book has been to present accounts of support, survival, and success of African-American elders based on their experiences.

Support networks were built based on strong religious ties that gave rise to partnerships between individuals in varied domains such as family, friends, and peer relationships. The strong religious ties of African Americans and the adherence to certain traditional beliefs can be respected and understood as responses to a long history of discrimination and oppression. Partnerships and other strong bonds were initiated not only out of basic survival but also out of concern and love for others.

This context of culture framed the belief systems of these African-American elders because of the absence of a structure within the larger society that is supportive of this ethnic group. The strong belief in God, church, family, friends, community, and self served as a foundation for the provision of basic survival strategies as well as ongoing support for a positive outlook on life.

The support process used by these elders reflected the unique meanings they attached to the support received from supportive others as well as the support given to others. Meanings reflected the need for establishing and nurturing close relationships that lasted over time. Listening, more specifically active listening, and availability rated quite high on the list. Other meanings included dependability, trust, respect, and passing the torch.

The worth of a soul, linking the past, present, and future, blessings, and change and challenges were all quite unique and added knowledge to the theoretical understanding of the social support process. Identification of the structure that supported and gave meaning to the beliefs of this group of elders is quite rewarding.

Memory is the ability to retain information over time. Time has been very generous to these elders. Elders store an unlimited number of memories over an extended period of time ranging from 70 to 99 years. These elders shared an array of memories that were mostly positive, yet some presented unique challenges. However, challenges were faced with grace and style. Lemons were used to make lemonade, and stumbling blocks were turned into stepping stones.

Colorful memories remained colorfast (they have not faded or changed in quality or significance). With grace and style, elders retrieved these memories upon command to effect the needed support, survival, and success.

Situations were faced and fixed. Sails were adjusted to navigate through strong winds. Sadness was avoided because elders did not fall prey to worrying; rather, they found peace and contentment in the midst of change and challenges. The positive choices allowed elders to conserve the physical, mental, and emotional energies necessary to persist.

REFERENCES

Antonucci, T. C. (1990). Social Supports and Social Relationships. In R. H. Binstock & L. K. George (Eds.). *Handbook of Aging and the Social Sciences* (3rd ed., pp. 205-226). San Diego: Academic Press.

Antonucci, T. C., & Akiyama, H. (1991). Convoys of Social Support: Generational issues. *Marriage and Family Review,* 16, 103-124.

Antonucci, T. C., & Akiyama, H. (1993). Stress and Coping in the Elderly. *Applied and Preventive Psychology,* 2, 201-208.

Atchley, R. C. (2003). *Social Forces and Aging: An Introduction to Social Gerontology* (9th ed.). Belmont, CA: Wadsworth.

Bee, H. L., & Bjorkland, B. R. (2004). *The Journey of Adulthood* (5th ed.). Upper Saddle River, NJ: Pearson Prentice Hall.

Bowers, C. A., & Gesten, E. L. (1986). Social Support as a Buffer of Anxiety: An Experimental Analogue. *American Journal of Community Psychology,* 14, 447-451.

Chatters, L. M., Taylor, R. J., & Jackson, J. S. (1985). Size and Composition of the Informal Helper Network of Elderly Blacks. *Journal of Gerontology*, 40, 605-614.

Chatters, L. M., Taylor, R. J., & Jackson, J. S. (1986). Aged Blacks' Choice for an Informer Helper Network. *Journal of Gerontology*, 41, 94-100.

Cobb, S. (1976). Social Support as a Moderator of Life Stress. *Psychosomatic Medicine*, 38, 300-314.

Coke, M. M. (1992). Correlates of Life Satisfaction Among Elderly African Americans. *Journal of Gerontology,* 47, P316-320.

Coke, M. M. & Twaite, J. A. (1995). *The Black Elderly: Satisfaction and Quality of Later Life.* New York: The Haworth Press.

Cutrona, C. E., & Suhr, J. A. (1994). Social Support Communication in the Context of Marriage: An Analysis of Couples' Supportive Interactions. In B. Burleson, T. Albrecht, & I. Sarason (Eds.), *Communication of Social Support: Messages, Interactions, Relationships, and Community* (pp. 113-135). Thousand Oaks: Sage.

Dressler, W. W. (1991). Social Support, Lifestyle Incongruity, and Arterial Blood Pressure in a Southern Black Community. *Psychosomatic Medicine*, 53, 608-620.

Erikson, E. H. (1982). *The Life Cycle Completed.* New York: Norton.

Hawks, S. R., Hull, M. L., Thalman, R. L., & Rickins, P. M. (1995). Review of Spiritual Health: Definition, Role and Intervention Strategies in Health Promotion. *American Journal of Health Promotion*, 9, 373-378.

Hildreth, G. J., Boglin, M. L., & Mask, K. (2000). Review of Literature on Resiliency in Black Families: Implications for the 21st Century. *African American Research Perspectives*, 6 (1), 13-21.

Hillier, S., & Barrow, G. W. (1999). *Aging: The Individual and Society*. Belmont, CA: Wadsworth Publishing Company.

Jackson, J. S., Chatters, L. M., & Taylor, R. J. (1993). Roles and Resources of the Black Elderly. In J. S. Jackson, L. M. Chatters, & R. J. Taylor (Eds.), *Aging in Black America* (pp. 1-18). Newbury Park: Sage.

Johnson, C. L., & Barer, B. M. (1990). Families and Networks Among Older Inner-city Blacks. *The Gerontologist*, 30, 726-733.

Jones, J. (1998). Examining the Concept of African-American Worship as Pertaining to Its Characteristics. An unpublished dissertation at Boston University, Boston, MA: Ann Arbor, MI: CMI.

Kahn, R. L. (1994). Social Support: Content, Causes and Consequences. In R. P. Abeles, H. C. Gift, & M. G. Ory (Eds.), *Aging and Quality of Life* (pp. 163-184). New York: Springer.

Krause, N., & Keith, V. (1989). Gender Differences in Social Support Among Older Adults. *Sex Roles*, 21, 609-628.

Lazarus, R. S., & Folkman, S. (1984). *Stress, Appraisal, and Coping*. New York: Springer.

Levin, J. S., & Taylor, R. J. (1993). Gender and Age Differences in Religiosity Among Black Americans. *The Gerontologist*, 33, 16-23.

Littlejohn-Blake, S. M., & Darling, C. A. (1993). Understanding the Strengths of African-American Families. *Journal of Black Studies*, 23, 460-471.

McAdoo, H. P. (1995). African-American Families: Strengths and Realities. In H. I. McCubbin, E. A. Thompson, A. I. Thompson, & J. A. Futrell (Eds.), *Resiliency in Ethnic Minority Families: African American Families, Volume 2*, (pp. 17-30). Madison: University of Wisconsin System.

McCubbin, H. I., Futrell, J. A., Thompson, E. A., & Thompson, A. I. (1995). Resilient Families in an Ethnic and Cultural Context. In H. I. McCubbin, E. A. Thompson, A. I. Thompson, & J. A. Futrell (Eds.), *Resiliency in Ethnic Minority Families: African-American Families, Volume 2*, (pp. 329-351). Madison: University of Wisconsin System.

Moss, G. E. (1973). *Illness, Immunity, and Social Interaction*. New York: Wiley.

Pollard, A. B. (1994). To Their Memory and Inspiration: Women, Men and the African American Church. *The A. M. E. Church Review*, 354, 32-35.

Pollard, A. B. (1995, November). Race, Religion, and Resistance in the African American Experience. Paper presented at the Associacao Nacional Casa Dandara International Seminar, Minas Gerais, Brazil.

Rosenthal, C. J. (1986). Family Supports in Later Life: Does Ethnicity Make a Difference? *The Gerontologist*, 26, 19-24.

Rubinstein, R. L., Lubben, J. E., & Mintzer, J. E. (1994). Social Isolation and Social Support: An Applied Perspective. *Journal of Applied Gerontology*, 13, 58-72.

Russell, D. W., & Cutrona, C. E. (1991). Social Support, Stress, and Depressive Symptoms Among the Elderly: Test of a Process Model. *Psychology and Aging*, 6, 190-201.

Smith, J. M. (1993). Function and Supportive Roles of Church and Religion. In J. S. Jackson, L. M. Chatters, & R. J. Taylor (Eds.), *Aging in Black America* (pp. 124-147). Newbury Park: Sage.

Stoller, E. P., & Pugliesi, K. L. (1991). Size and Effectiveness of Informal Networks: A Panel Study of Older People in the Community. *Journal of Health and Social Behavior*, 33, 180-191.

Streeter, C., & Franklin, C. (1992). Defining and Measuring Social Support: Guidelines for Social Work Practitioners. *Research on Social Work Practice*, 2, 81-98.

Sutherland, M., Hale, C. D., & Harris, G. T. (1995). Community Health Promotion: The Church as Partner. *Journal of Primary Prevention*, 16, 201-217.

Taylor, R. J. (1986). Receipt of Support from Family Among Black Americans: Demographics and Familial Differences. *Journal of Marriage and the Family*, 48, 67-77.

Taylor, R. J., & Chatters, L. M. (1986). Patterns of Informal Support to Elderly Black Adults: Family, Friends, and Church Members. *Social Work*, 31, 432-438.

Taylor, R. J., & Chatters, L. M. (1988). Church Members as a Source of Informal Social Support. *Review of Religious Research*, 30, 193-203.

Taylor, R. J., & Chatters, L. M. (1991). Extended Family Networks of Older Adults. *Journal of Gerontology*, 46, S210-217.

Thoits, P. A. (1982). Conceptual, Methodological, and Theoretical Problems in Studying Social Support as a Buffer Against Life Stress. *Journal of Health and Social Behavior*, 23, 145-159.

Thoits, P. A. (1995). Stress, Coping, and Social Support Processes: Where Are We? What Next? *Journal of Health and Social Behavior*, (Extra Issue), 53-79.

Walls, C. T. & Zarit, S. H. (1991). Informal Support from Black Churches and the Well-being of Elderly Blacks. *The Gerontologist*, 31, 490-495.

Ward, R. A. (1985). Informal Networks and Well-being in Later Life: A Research Agenda. *The Gerontologist*, 25, 55-61.

Wimberly, A. S. (Ed.). (1997). *Honoring African American Elders: A Ministry in the Soul Community*. San Francisco: Jossey-Bass.

Glossary

Acceptance - Approval or confirmation.

Action Facilitating - Providing information and tangible aid to someone to assist with solving a problem.

Aging - The condition of becoming mature or old. Progressing through the various life stages (i.e., childhood, youth, young adulthood, late adulthood).

B

Being There - Being flexible, available, and willing to provide assistance as needed without reservation.

Beliefs - A system or structure of convictions based on reality or truth (i.e., doctrines, rituals, creeds, faith).

Bible Reading - A regular schedule of examining the Scriptures for inspiration and understanding.

Birthing - Bringing forth, causing, creating, or originating components of a relationship.

Blessings - Positive results or special benefits realized from good wishes, happiness, or approval.

Business - Attention to needs, goals, and objectives.

C

Challenges - Situations or events requiring proof, explanation, special efforts or dedication.

Change - To alter or replace; to make a substitution or transformation.

Christian Principles - Standards exemplifying the qualities of love, kindness, decency, and humility.

Cohorts - Individuals sharing common events, such as birth year, historical periods, social settings, or income level.

Confusion - A state of chaos, disconnection, or disorder.

Consequences - Direct results of actions through cause and effect.

Contentment - A feeling of ease and comfort.

D

Dependability - Trustworthy and reliable behavior.

Do Unto Others - Turnabout; fair play; to put forth one's best efforts to bring to a just completion.

E

Extended Family - Individuals connected to a nuclear family and living in proximity or the same dwelling.

F

Family - Individuals usually related by blood (biological) and/or marriage (spouse).

Fellowship - Shared activities in a social setting.

Flexibility - The ability to make modifications and exercise fluidity without becoming rigid.

Formal Support - Structured, systematic, or fixed rules, customs, or criteria.

Friends - Associates or close acquaintances who share common concerns, interests, and ideas.

Future - Approaching time.

G

Gender - Classification of male or female (often in relation to self-esteem, social status, and goals).

Give - Contribute goods and/or services to others, not necessarily for remuneration.

Give-and-take - Exchanging on an even basis.

Gratitude - An expression of pleasure, satisfaction, and thankfulness for benefits received.

I

Informal Support - Support that is casual, relaxed, and not governed by established rules or customs.

Internet Information Resources - Websites that provide links to aging programs and services.

Intimacy - Close association or familiarity.

J

Joy - Exhilaration and positive energy or pleasure because of accomplishments or goals achieved.

L

Life's Lessons - Special instructions to be learned over a given period of time.

Like Family - Persons who provide moral and social support typically provided by biological relatives.

Linking - Connecting or joining together.

Listening - Giving attention to spoken words; making a conscious effort to pay close attention, so as to hear.

Long-lasting Relationships - Relationships and/or connections sustained over a lengthy span of time.

M

Meanings - Purpose or descriptions ascribed or assigned to acts, events, situations, or relationships.

Mental Well-being - Emotional stability and peace of mind.

Minding My Own Business - Refraining from infringing on or violating the rights and privacy of others.

Most Supportive Others - Persons providing support without coercion or promise of reward or incentive.

N

Neighbor - An individual residing in proximity or association with others within a common community or living area.

Nurturant - One who provides comfort and consolation without solving problems.

Nurturing - Promoting development through training and education.

P

Past - Prior time or events that are bygone.

Peace - A state of calm and quiet, free from confusion and frustration.

Positive Outlook - A confident and assured demeanor.

Praying - The act of talking to God in praise, confession, or thanksgiving.

Present - The here and now; that which is current and in progress.

Pride - Delight or satisfaction in the achievements or accomplishments of self and/or others.

Priorities - Some things that are considered to be more important than everything else.

Privacy - Confidentiality; secrecy.

R

Relationships - Continuing associations or attachments between individuals.

Respect - Esteem, high regard, or honor.

Responsibility - The state of having dependability or accountability regarding obligations.

Rituals - Customs and traditions observed at designated times.

Rules - Prescribed practices to be followed.

S

Social Support - The emotional sustenance and practical assistance provided in times of need by people, or groups of people, with close personal ties.

Sticking Together - Remaining faithful or loyal to friends, family, associates, and acquaintances.

Supportive Others - Persons available to provide assistance without obligation.

T

Take - To capture or claim possession of.

Thankfulness - Gratitude.

The Golden Rule - "Treat others as one desires to be treated."

Torch - Any source of illumination, inspiration, or enlightenment.

Training - The method of preparing others for service or duty.

Trust - Honesty, integrity.

U

Unity - Togetherness or collaboration in reaching a common goal.

W

Well-being - Positive emotional, mental, physical, and spiritual health, contentment, and/or prosperity.

Wisdom - Good judgment based on knowledge, skills, experience, and understanding.

Worry - A state of instability based on anxiety, annoyance, trials, and difficulties.

Y

Yesteryears - Days past and gone.

Internet Information Resources

http://www.aarp.org

AARP - Information, advocacy, and benefits for people age 50 and over. (Services include care and family, community service, learning and technology, health and wellness, money and work, policy and research, travel and leisure, and other links.)

http://www.ageinfo.org

Resources for Aging: The Caregiver Sourcebook. (Elder care, caregiving, retirement planning, elder law, Medicare, Medicaid, assisted living, hospice, adult day care, behavioral health, respite, many other services, and other links.)

http://www.agework.com

AgeWork Career Center. (The one-stop shop to jobs in the field of aging, major resources, and other links.)

http://www.alz.org

Alzheimer's Association. (Information and discussion on Alzheimer's disease, caregiving, referrals, and other links.)

http://www.aoa.gov

AoA - Administration on Aging - Department of Health and Human Services. (Services regarding elders and families, professionals, Medicare updates, top stories, aging news, features, and other links.)

http://www.aoa.dhhs.gov/aoa/pages/jpost/st.html

Administration on Aging: Department of Health and Human Services. (Listing of Internet resources on aging.)

http://www.apa.org

American Psychological Association. (News, publications, research, topics, monthly newsletter, and quick links.)

http://www.arthritis.org

Arthritis Foundation. (Resources, communities, events and programs, conditions and treatment, advocacy, research, and other links.)

http://www.asaging.org

American Society on Aging - Enhancing the knowledge and skills of those working with older adults. (Conferences, publications, resources, events, job board, and other links.)

http://www.benefitscheckup.org

NCOA - A service of the National Council on the Aging—Benefits Check-up. (Medicare, prescription drugs, property taxes, bills, meals, and other links.)

http://www.blackamericaweb.com

Black America Web. (News, leisure and fun, praise and inspiration, health, career, finance, Tom Joyner Foundation, and other links.)

http://www.caregiver.org

FCA: Family Caregiver Alliance - National Center on Caregiving. (Public policy and research, caregiving information and advice, fact sheets and publications, newsletters, groups, and other links.)

http://www.careersinaging.com

Careers in Aging. (Services include information, programs, brochures, newsletters, displays and career fairs regarding careers in aging, and other links.)

http://www.dol.gov

U.S. Department of Labor. (Resources and links to pension information and other links.)

http://www.dukespiritualityandhealth.org

Center for the Study of Religion/Spirituality and Health. (Research, medical education, speaking engagements, books, news, and other links.)

http://www.eldercare.org

Resources on Elder Care Services. (Home care, aging, disabilities, senior housing, advocacy, Medicare, health insurance, counseling, and other links.)

http://www.elderfriends.org

ElderFriends. (Relieving isolation and loneliness among older adults, independence, and other links.)

http://www.elderweb.com

ELDERWEB. (Information for older adults and caregivers and other links.)

http://www.familiesusa.org

Families USA: The Voice for Health Care Consumers. (Issues, resources, Medicaid, Medicare, health action, employment, and other links.)

http://www.geron.org

The Gerontological Society of America. (Research, education, practice, career center, and other links.)

http://www.hud.gov

U.S. Department of Housing and Urban Development. (Information regarding housing policy or programs.)

http://www.infoaging.org

American Federation for Aging Research. (Disease center, biology of aging, healthy aging, nutrition information center, news, ask the expert, research spotlight, and other links.)

http://www.medscape.com

Medscape from WebMD. (Resource centers, conference coverage, patient education, library, discussions, specialty home pages, and other links.)

http://www.nahc.org

National Association for Home Care. (Information about state organizations, consumer information, policy and other legislative issues, and other links.)

http://www.ncba-aged.org/health

National Caucus and Center on Black Aged, Inc. (Resources, policy issues, publications, programs, information and referral, prevention and control of chronic diseases, emphasizing cancer [prostate, colorectal, breast, and cervical], diabetes, cardiovascular disease, and other links.)

http://www.nia.gov

National Institute on Aging. (Health information, research information, news and events, and other links.)

http://www.nih.gov

U. S. Department of Health and Human Services, National Institutes of Health. (Health, news, institutes, health issues, medical research issues, and other links.)

http://www.nsclc.org

National Senior Citizens Law Center. (Older Americans Act; Information on Medicare, SSI, Medicaid, Social Security, mandatory retirement, age discrimination, and other links.)

http://www.seniorlaw.com

Senior Law Home Page. (Specialists in elder law and other links.)

http://www.seniorlink.com

Senior Link Online. (Elder care resource; consultation and referral for older adults, families, caregivers, and other links.)

http://www.ssa.gov

Social Security Administration. (Review earnings, statistical information, benefits, beneficiaries, legislative changes, etc.)

http://www.seniorservices.org

Supporting the independence of seniors. (News, senior issues, and other links.)

http://www.seniors-site.com

The website for senior citizens and adults 50+, their children and caregivers. (Special offers, message boards, aging concerns, financial information, and other links.)

http://www.seniorworld.com

Resources for active seniors in the digital age. (Health, home and garden, money, life, leisure and sports, real estate, travel and recreation, news and opinions, arts and entertainment, featured articles, and other links.)

http://www.spirituality.org

Spirituality for Today - A Christian Faith Magazine. (Thoughts for the week, faith, prayer, and other links.)

http://www.usda.gov

United States Department of Agriculture. (Agriculture, education and outreach, food and nutrition, laws and regulations, travel and recreation, and other links.)

http://www.visionaryproject.com

National Visionary Leadership Project. The mission is to ensure that the wisdom of extraordinary African American elders is preserved and passed to the leaders of tomorrow. (Fellowship program, chat room, message board, newsletter, and other links.)

Scriptures

Name Index

P

R

S

T

W

Z

Subject Index

A

B

C

D

E

F

www.ingramcontent.com/pod-product-compliance
Lightning Source LLC
LaVergne TN
LVHW020635100826
845148LV00012B/2196

* 9 7 8 1 5 8 9 4 2 3 5 1 0 *